BEESON
PASTORAL SERIES

TAKING RISKS IN MINISTRY

DALE GALLOWAY
AND BEESON INSTITUTE COLLEAGUES

Beacon Hill Press of Kansas City
Kansas City, Missouri

ISBN 083-411-9811

Printed in the
United States of America

Cover Design: Paul Franitza

All Scripture quotations not otherwise designated are from the *Holy Bible, New International Version*® (NIV®). Copyright © 1973, 1978, 1984 by International Bible Society. Used by permission of Zondervan Publishing House. All rights reserved.

Permission to quote from the following additional copyrighted versions of the Bible is acknowledged with appreciation:

New American Standard Bible (NASB®), © copyright The Lockman Foundation 1960, 1962, 1963, 1968, 1971, 1972, 1973, 1975, 1977, 1995.

The *New King James Version* (NKJV). Copyright © 1979, 1980, 1982 Thomas Nelson, Inc.

The *New Revised Standard Version* (NRSV) of the Bible, copyright 1989 by the Division of Christian Education of the National Council of the Churches of Christ in the USA. All rights reserved.

The Living Bible (TLB), © 1971. Used by permission of Tyndale House Publishers, Inc., Wheaton, IL 60189. All rights reserved.

The Message (TM). Copyright © 1993, 1994, 1995, 1996, 2000, 2001, 2002. Used by permission of NavPress Publishing Group.

Library of Congress Cataloging-in-Publication Data

Taking risks in ministry / Dale Galloway and Beeson Institute colleagues.
    p. cm. — (Beeson pastoral series)
Includes bibliographical references.
  ISBN 0-8341-1981-1
  1. Church work. I. Galloway, Dale E. II. Series.

BV4400 .T35 2003
253—dc21

                                                              2002152769

10 9 8 7 6 5 4 3 2 1

Contents

PREFACE   5

ACKNOWLEDGMENTS   7

1 PREVAILING FAITH   9
  The Extra Edge for Facing Risks
  Dale Galloway

2 RISKY MISSION AT COMMUNITY CHURCH OF JOY   25
  Safe and Sound or Dangerous and Exciting?
  Walt Kallestad

3 ARE WE DOING WHAT WE'RE SAYING?   37
  Challenging Churches to Go on Mission with Jesus
  Bill Easum

4 MINIMIZING THE DOWNSIDE OF RISK   45
  Recruiting and Developing the Right Staff
  Leith Anderson

5 RISKING A CULTURE OF CREATIVITY   53
  Creativity, Efficiency, and Effectiveness
  Leith Anderson

6 PLANNING WORSHIP THE WAY WE'VE NEVER   65
  DONE IT BEFORE
  Giving Worship to the People
  Sally Morgenthaler

7 GREAT LEADERS TAKE RISKS   77
  Knowing What Risks to Take When
  Elmer Towns

8 RISKS REQUIRED IN TURNAROUND CHURCHES   93
  Disciple-Making Is the Key
  Bill Easum

9 HOW TO RAISE MONEY AND FAITH WITHOUT SINKING   107
THE SHIP
Making God Your Source
Dale Galloway

10 HEALTHY RELATIONSHIPS: THE FOUNDATION   115
FOR RISK-TAKING
The Art and Heart of 21st-Century Leadership
Wayne Cordeiro

11 TAKING RISKS WITHOUT RISKING YOUR SOUL   123
The Pastor-Leader's Need for a Healthy Soul
Maxie Dunnam

Preface

I have observed over the years that a fine line exists between foolishness and risking in faith. We've all seen people do things that they call faith that appeared to be very foolish and ended up with bad results.

Two different mental pictures have helped me understand the difference between the two. Foolishness is like jumping off a tall building. Laws of gravity inevitably cause the jumper to get severely hurt and likely die. By contrast, risking in faith is like climbing steps one at a time. When you reach the step God has led you to take next, then "risking faith" is the stretch needed to go to the next step. The person who exercises risk-taking faith is like someone climbing steps—ever stretching and ever reaching toward the next step.

In this book we tried to select persons who are examples of risking faith to give you a better understanding of how God wants you to reach beyond where you are to go to the next place of ministry.

R isking in faith is like climbing
steps one at a time.

My opening chapter, "Prevailing Faith," roots the idea in the gallery of faith found in Heb. 11 and 12. Walt Kallestad (chapter 2) and Wayne Cordeiro (chapter 10) provide outstanding case studies of churches that took major risks of faith. Bill Easum challenges us to make faith a way of life (chapters 3 and 8), and Elmer Towns shows how good leadership regularly takes risks (chapter 7). Leith Anderson illustrates how his church minimizes the downside of risk both in its staffing and in the culture it develops (chapters 4 and 5). Sally Morgenthaler applies the idea of risk-taking faith to our worship services (chapter 6), and I apply the role of risk-taking faith to funding the vision (chapter 9). Finally, Maxie Dunnam puts everything in perspective with the challenge of "Taking Risks Without Risking Your Soul" (chapter 11).

One of my lifetime quotes that I've affirmed through the years comes from something Robert Schuller says constantly: "I'd rather attempt something great for God and fail than to try nothing at all." May you, too, trust God by taking bold risks of faith.

Acknowledgments

The first generation of Christians took risks of faith to spread the gospel into new places and new cultures. Many succeeding generations of disciples also took risks, which led ultimately to my own transformed life in Christ. I then continued to follow that model as I pastored two established churches and launched two new churches, and now as I mentor Beeson pastors to become leaders of leaders.

I'm thankful for each of those risk-taking people who went before me, having an influence on my life. I pray that my wife, Margi, and I never stop taking risks of faith.

I'm also thankful for each of the contributors to this book, who likewise have helped me in my journey. Each one is a personal friend and a source of great inspiration.

Warren Bird from my office and Neil Wiseman from the Beacon Hill offices have done a great deal of work to transform the chapters that follow from spoken presentations into written documents. Penny Ruot, Ellen Frisius, Heather McPherson, and others have assisted from the Beeson Center office.

The Beeson Institute for Advanced Church Leadership, from which these messages originated, is a field-based coaching relationship designed to accelerate the gift development of senior pastors who want to grow strong, healthy, and effective churches. To date, several hundred have already completed the training. Several hundred others are current participants. My prayer for all of them is that they continue to become the daring risk-takers of faith described in this book.

To join this three-times-a-year gathering, call toll-free 888-5BEESON or E-mail <Beeson_Institute@asburyseminary.edu>.

▪1▪
PREVAILING FAITH
The Extra Edge for Facing Risks
Dale Galloway

Leaders in the business community constantly look for an extra edge for building great corporations that produce healthy profits. Daniel Goleman's writings on *Emotional Intelligence* and Jim Collins' concept of "level five" leadership in his book *Good to Great* offer some significant insights about the extra edge for business leaders. In similar ways, churches desiring to be all they can be keep looking for an extra edge to increase their effectiveness. Far from being new, taking full advantage of prevailing faith is our extra edge. Taking full advantage of prevailing faith fuels an attitude I see in effective churches that says, "We're willing to risk. We'd rather attempt something great for God than to do nothing at all—and succeed!"

Realistically, every great accomplishment for God involves risks for someone or some group. Interesting enough, for our inspiration as well as our challenge, we must realize every great accomplishment in Christian history stands as a silent witness to how much the Father honors prevailing faith in His children. Those who never risk never accomplish much for God. And at the end of their years of service, they look back with regret because, in an ultimate sense, playing it safe never satisfies.

Though not speaking directly to the church, Jawaharlal Nehru, the first prime minister of India, has 12 brief words church leaders need to hear and heed, "The policy of being too cautious is the greatest risk of all" (John Woods, ed., *The Quotable Executive,* 197).

From my repeated devotional reading of Heb. 11 and 12, I have come to believe a two-word phrase—*prevailing faith*—sums up these lofty chapters. That's the extra edge for a church and her leaders. Worthwhile risk plus prevailing faith add up to Kingdom achievement.

More than 150 years ago, Danish philosopher Søren Kierkegaard came to a similar conclusion: "Without risk there is no faith, and the greater the risk, the greater the faith" (Rebecca Davis, ed., *The Treasury of Religious and Spiritual Quotations*, 1994], 494).

Whenever you find a great church—a transforming church, a cutting-edge church—you find a leader and followers who through prevailing faith are willing to risk for God.

According to the Bible, our faith connected with God's power produces extraordinary results. Many characteristics of prevailing faith almost jump off the pages of the Bible from Heb. 11 and 12. To achieve more for God, we need to deepen our understanding of prevailing faith. Do you have dreams to make your life and service for Christ really count but wonder how to do it? The following biblical principles will get you started.

1. The Prevailing Faith Leader Stays Focused on Jesus

The strength of our faith comes from Jesus, not ourselves. The writer to the Hebrews tells us that what Jesus did at the cross is our motivation for risking faith: "Let us fix our eyes on Jesus, the author and perfecter of our faith, who for the joy set before him endured the cross" (12:2). Ponder the connection, if you can, between joy and enduring the Cross.

In partnership with Jesus, I become more, so much more, than I could be by my own efforts.

Only by focusing our minds and wills on Jesus can we lead people beyond where they never dreamed they could go or help them see spiritual potential they've never imagined.

In partnership with Jesus, I become more, so much more, than I could be by my own efforts. In Christ I find the strength beyond my own to ask people to join me in doing things for God that I would never ask if it weren't for the all-consuming dream God has given me. In his book *The Arc of Ambition,* James Champy calls this "the enormous appeal of a worthwhile case" (118). Jesus is the ultimate attraction of His Church.

Is it not true that every effective leader sometimes feels inadequate? Moses felt deficient about his speech and his leadership. Yet God used him to lead the children of Israel out of Egypt. Even though he felt incapable, he kept focused on God's enabling power. He learned that lesson well a long time before Paul wrote, "I can do all things through Christ who strengthens me" (Phil. 4:13, NKJV). To this day, Jesus stands as a giant among the heroes of faith listed in Heb. 11. The effective church keeps focused on her living Lord.

2. The Prevailing Faith Leader Is a Visionary

Vision has always held high priorities for achievers—especially leaders in the Church. English poet, political writer, and clergyman Jonathan Swift, who lived near the end of the 1600s, said it in a short, timeless sentence: "Vision is the art of seeing things invisible." Carl Sandberg, the American poet who lived into the first half of the last century, adds another significant dimension to what it means to be a visionary: "Nothing happens unless there is first a dream." But beyond the insights of Swift and Sandberg, the writer to the Hebrews stretches our concepts when he ties vision and faith together: "Now faith is a substance of things hoped for, the evidence of things not seen" (11:1, NKJV).

Vision is faith with a picture attached.

Vision is faith with a picture attached. The visionary leader sees what others do not see, sees before others, sees what may not even exist, and sees the results of following a vision. Authentic visionary leaders communicate a picture of a preferred future that people can see, believe, and support.

I remember sitting in a Denny's restaurant many years ago, along with Glen Cole and Denny Davis. All three of us were pastors who were impacted by a young visionary leader named Robert Schuller. He had convened either the first or second Institute for Schuller Successful Church Leadership. Though only 75 church leaders attended, the conference provided a context that enabled us to dream and to verbalize it.

The three of us, who have since become longtime friends, shared our dreams that night. We talked about what a great church would look like. We made commitments that we were going to spend our lives bringing to reality the vision God had given us for building a great church. Twenty years later, God had done it. But first we had to see the picture of what could be.

At that same institute, my wife, Margi, also caught the vision for our work in Portland. I had resigned an established church and was dreaming of starting a new congregation to reach thousands of the unchurched in that great Northwestern city. As we sat in Schuller's Tower of Hope, I asked God to give Margi the vision for our future together. God answered that prayer, and we have become partners in the vision and its achievement across these years.

A few years later at yet another Schuller Institute, I recall sitting over coffee with Sundo Kim. He shared his dream for a great prevailing faith church in Korea. In the years that followed, he built what has become the world's largest church for his denomination.

3. The Prevailing Faith Leader Is a Pioneer

As a pioneer, the prevailing faith leader never settles for the status quo. Pioneers challenge processes, situations, difficulties, and present realities. They believe the church can be relevant, alive, and able to help sinners be transformed into saints. Like American frontier leaders, these spiritual leaders test boundaries and make amazing discoveries about God in the process.

Notice the cutting-edge, move-toward-the-future spirit of this verse: "By faith Abraham obeyed when he was called to go out to the place which he would receive as an inheritance. And he went out, not knowing where he was going" (Heb. 11:8, NKJV). Though people of great faith do not always know where they're going, they know who they are going with. They know God is with them and that their dependence is Him.

Great automobile genius Henry Ford shared this insight from his own experience as leader in the auto industry: "One of the greatest discoveries a man can make, one of the greatest surprises, is to find he can do what he is afraid to do." Pioneers discover that God is often ready to do through them what they were afraid to try by themselves.

ike the trapeze artist, one rope has to be released before the other one comes into our hands.

For a genuine pioneer, risking faith means leaving something to receive something better. Like the trapeze artist, one rope has to be released before the other one comes into our hands. One unknown writer called it the agony of the in-between life.

When I launched New Hope Community Church, it meant leaving friends, giving up material security, turning my back on the church of my childhood, and putting behind me many other things to which I was emotionally attached. But what an adventure! I wouldn't have missed it for anything.

Why not move ahead to reach to new horizons? Listen to your pioneer heart. And experience the thrill of being a person of prevailing faith.

May these words, that mean so much to me, become your heartbeat:

> *Grieve not for me, about to start a new adventure.*
> *Eager I stand, and ready to depart,*
> *Me and my reckless pioneer heart*
> —Author unknown

4. The Prevailing Faith Leader Is an Entrepreneur

Can you see and feel the entrepreneurial spirit in the following verse? "By faith we understand that the worlds were framed by the word of God so the things which are seen were not made of things which are visible" (Heb. 11:3, NKJV).

God, the Master Craftsman, not only created the world but also invented creativity and imagination and the ability to dream for Kingdom achievement. Risky faith was His idea long before any of us thought about it.

God shares His creativeness each time He uses one of us to develop something new. His shared creativity gives us new ways to reach people, new strategies for training leaders, or a plan for a new kind of worship service. To be a prevailing faith leader, we must seek and use the creative enablement of God in the details of our ministry assignment.

> *isky faith was God's idea long before any of us ever thought about it.*

For example, I learned new paradigms for evangelism, each of which helped me reach many more people than in my previous ways. As a young pastor, the only way I knew how to start a church was by holding revival meetings and knocking on doors. I went door to door inviting people to church, but I did not know how to talk with them on a one-on-one basis about spiritual things.

As I mention often in my writing and preaching, a creative entrepreneurial spirit started to develop in me when I tried to think of innovative methods of evangelism. It started one day when I met a Campus Crusade for Christ staffer at a nearby university who sketched on a napkin what many know as the "four spiritual laws." That afternoon I went back to my suburb of Columbus, Ohio, and led two people to faith in Christ, using the napkin as my guide. This was a great new paradigm for me.

Recently when I visited that congregation, I met 25 families who came to Christ through my personal evangelism efforts in that congregation three decades before. What a payoff for implementing a "new" idea.

Later I learned about using small groups to reach people. The basic idea goes back to John Wesley, who shared his ministry with group leaders and in the process helped them grow strong spiritually even as they served others. The outreach potential and the discipleship possibilities of small groups are enormous.

At another time in my pastoral journey, I came across the idea of a "Pastor's Welcome Class." This class is for newcomers and outsiders who have little knowledge of the church. Over the years, I saw hundreds of people come to Christ through that class at New Hope.

Create a climate in your church in which people are encouraged to be innovative and given the opportunity to carry out their dreams.

Create a climate in your church in which people are encouraged to be innovative and given the opportunity to carry out their dreams—and to try new ministries. Then many will be challenged and stretched. God will energize them. As a result, the church will prosper and grow. Prevailing faith creates churches that are spiritually strong and robust in winning new people.

5. The Prevailing Faith Leader Gathers People

If you want to build a great church, you must gather lots of people. You have to be consumed from early morning until late at night with a passion to reach new people and a commitment to strengthen the people of God. To build a great people-focused church, you personally must keep reaching out to individuals until you have assembled 400 to 500 people. The majority of your waking moments must go to thinking and asking, "How do we gather people?"

Once you have gathered that many relationally connected people who are excited about serving Jesus, they will spark outreach and momentum to bring in hundreds or perhaps even thousands more. Once you reach that critical mass level, the people become gatherers of other people.

At that point you must commit yourself to learn new skills of leadership, such as how to manage success. Then you'll be forced to learn how to become more of a leader of leaders. Then you must be consumed with how to build the strongest staff possible.

God used Abraham's faith to raise up descendants "as numerous as the stars in the sky and as countless as the sand on the seashore" (Heb. 11:12). Likewise, a crowd that is enthusiastic for Jesus can bring about a huge spiritual multiplication effect on their community.

6. A Prevailing Faith Leader Is Someone Willing to Pay the Price

There is no feast without a sacrifice. Those who have prevailing faith are leaders who have given up their self-centeredness for something greater and much more satisfying—the cause of Christ. There is no effectiveness without some pain and often even some controversy.

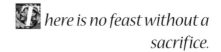 *here is no feast without a sacrifice.*

God commends people who are willing to pay a price motivated by faith: "By faith Abel offered God a better sacrifice than Cain did. By faith he was commended as a righteous man, when God spoke well of his offerings. And by faith he still speaks, even though he is dead" (Heb. 11:4).

In Heb. 11 we're reminded that Moses refused to live a life of ease by becoming the spoiled grandson of Pharaoh. He chose the more difficult way, and God honored his commitment, as He always does.

Abraham held nothing back from God. He obeyed God even to the point of being willing to offer Isaac, his son of promise, upon the altar of sacrifice.

In fact, any significant gain in life usually comes at some great cost to a leader. According to legendary Ohio State University football coach Woody Hayes, "There is nothing in the world that comes easy. There are a lot of people that aren't going to bother to win. We learn in football to get up and go once more."

That's the way it has to be in the church too. The leader pays a price of running further and harder and longer. He or she pays the price of running faster and for making something significant happen. But there's a rich payoff too. There's nothing greater than giving your life for the cause of Christ in building a prevailing faith church.

In ministry every effective pastor will be called to sacrifice, stretch, and grow. Let me explain why I believe this is true. I learned the hard way that I could never take the church to a new level of ministry without paying the price personally. Before I could lead the church deeper and further in the work of God, I had to go deeper in my own spiritual commitments, to develop new skills, and to release more authority to others.

I'm a much better Christian because of this Kingdom principle—each new level of ministry requires new levels of sacrifice and commitment of the leader. This is the delightful agony of achievement in the cause of Christ.

When my wife, Margi, and I were preparing to start New Hope Community Church, we had no outside backing. So I made a list of possibilities of people who might help us. I took my little green notebook that contained 23 names and visited each person to cast the vision and ask their help. When I was done, I still had no money. Not a single person had made a commitment to help when we started.

I had to make a decision about what to do. The problem was a lack of funds, but that was different from the decision I needed to make. Margi and I backed off and prayed, *Father, are You calling us to start a new outreach-focused church to reach the unchurched thousands of Portland with the positive, life-changing message of new hope in Jesus Christ?*

The answer was yes, but we didn't know how. Then we began thinking about our house. Margi's family had always lived in a parsonage. Our little "honeymoon cottage" was her first home. We had about $7,000 in equity in it. We sold and used the equity as our financial launch resource.

7. A Prevailing Faith Leader Is More like a Hedgehog than a Fox

In Jim Collins' book *Good to Great,* which I mentioned earlier in this chapter, he tells about Latvian-born English philosopher Isaiah Berlin's famous essay "The Hedgehog and the Fox." In the essay the author divides the world into hedgehogs and foxes based on an ancient Greek parable.

"The fox knows many things, but the hedgehog knows one big thing—that the fox is coming!" writes Berlin.

The fox is a cunning creature able to devise many sneak attacks on the hedgehog. Day after day the fox circles the hedgehog's den, waiting for the perfect moment to pounce. Fast and crafty, the fox looks like a sure winner.

On the other hand, the hedgehog looks like a sure loser. He waddles along, going about his simple daily tasks, searching for lunch, taking care of his home.

The fox thinks he's got him as he comes bounding across the ground in speedy pursuit. The hedgehog, sensing danger, looks up and says to himself, *Here we go again—will he ever learn?* Rolling up into a perfect little ball, the hedgehog becomes a sphere of sharp spikes pointing outward in all directions.

That's the highly desirable effect of focus for the church—direction, concentration, and desirable outcome.

Racing toward his prey, the fox sees the hedgehog's defense, calls off the attack, and retreats to the forest to calculate a new line of attack. Each day some version of this battle takes place. Despite the greater cunning of the fox, the hedgehog always wins.

Then Jim Collins asks, "Why does the hedgehog win?" (90-91). Its secret is focus.

Management specialist Ken Blanchard and Coach Don Shula have a lot to teach the church in what they say about focus in football: "Like those river banks, a good coach provides the direction and concentration for performers' energies, helping channel all their efforts toward a single desired outcome" (*The Little Book of Coaching*, 15). That's also the highly desirable effect of focus for the church—direction, concentration, and desirable outcome. Churches and spiritual leaders who are focused accomplish more and enjoy increased satisfaction in the process.

Sometimes people ask me how I created 500 small groups in a single church. Researchers say it was the largest number of small groups in any individual church in North America at that time.

I didn't do it in a day, a month, or a year. It took 23 years of focus. It started simply: I started a group, and my wife, Margi, started a group. We raised up leaders out of those groups and helped them start more groups. Out of those groups came more leaders, who started even more groups.

We experienced the cycle of accumulative effective service of Christ. New people would enter the groups. They would become Christians. They would become apprentice leaders. They would become leaders and start reaching new people through their new groups. I did that every day, week, and month. I added staff people who made leadership development their focus, and they kept at it year after year. There are many things in life I will never know how to do, but I do know how to stay focused. Like a magnifying glass lined up focused on the power of the sun, you can start fires all over. The power of focus produces amazing results.

Andy Stanley pastors North Point Community Church in northwest Atlanta. His leadership is an example of prevailing faith as he led his church to focus on what they call alignment. They know who they are and what God has called them to do. They continually ask, "Does this idea of potential new ministry align with our vision?" As a result, they focus on a few things that they do well. They say no to a lot of other opportunities. What they say no to gives them as much focus power as what they accept.

8. A Prevailing Faith Leader Is a Team Builder

To build a prevailing faith church, leaders have to work with others to build community and multiple ministry. An effective prevailing faith church is built by a team who work together—it is the gospel lived out in relationships and the gospel shared with those who do not yet know Christ.

Though he was not writing specifically for Christian readers, Lawrence Holpp offers an important directive for those who want to build a church team: "We all know what the word team means—'a number of individuals associated in some joint action,' the dictionary informs us. So we may not think any further. That's a big mistake. A team should be defined in terms of purpose, place, powers, plan and people" (*Managing Teams*, 4). And he's right. Any group who gives attention to those five words is well on its way to significant achievement as a team.

If God has given you a vision for the future achievement of the church you serve, you cannot achieve it alone, or else the dream is not big enough. Every vision from God is dependent upon your ability to build a team. The spelling of the word "team" could be viewed two different ways: Together Everyone Achieves More, or Together Everyone Achieves Miracles. Either way, the importance of a team idea gets communicated to the congregation. We really do need each other.

9. A Prevailing Faith Leader Finds Ways to Be an Overcomer

In addition to the call for adventure and the strength to overcome, Hebrews 11 contains a sobering message. Verses 36 to 38 describe the terrible opposition faced by people of faith—from jeers and flogging to death itself. They suffered, according to Scripture, to obtain "a better resurrection" (v. 35).

> *It's not what happens to you in
> the journey, but what happens
> inside of you.*

Like them, you will face obstacles, maybe not death or physical abuse, but changes that have to be renegotiated over and over again. These are frustrations that have to be endured in order to accomplish the mission.

God inspired Millard Fuller to create a whole movement to help poor people. He founded Habitat for Humanity, an organization that has built more than 100,000 homes for people who did not have a home previously. He says the organization is all about putting Jesus' love into action. Though I never met Millard Fuller, I have talked with enough leaders to be confident that Habitat for Humanity, like every Kingdom-related organization, has hit snags, obstacles, and even dead ends.

The more worthwhile your dreams, the more setbacks you will face. How you handle foot-dragging and attacks will determine more of your effectiveness in ministry in the long run than anything else you do. It's not what happens *to* you in the journey, but what happens *inside* of you. God uses the testings to refine you and develop you for an even greater future.

Those with prevailing faith learn to hold steady in the storm.

When I was 10 years old, I went on a fishing trip with my family to Minnesota. One day the men went about 30 miles out with a guide. That day my job was to remain local and stay with my mother and three other women who appointed me boat captain to take them fishing.

We went a couple of miles out on the lake, and a terrible storm hit. The waves began rolling into the boat, and I became scared. My dad had taught me not to panic. You head the boat into the waves toward the shore. The women were praying, and I was shaking, but I kept it steady until we reached the shore safely.

In ministry, storms hit you. They come by way of staff difficulties, leadership issues, financial crises, or any number of other frightening winds. In the first eight years of ministry at New Hope when we rented facilities, we were sold out of one place, burned out of another, and kicked out of two others.

What I learned: In every adversity, look for the hidden opportunity. The Adventist church building that we were using in the early days of New Hope Community Church had a fire and became unusable. We needed a new place immediately. I had been in discussion with a local college to use their chapel, but the president wanted a lot more money than we could pay. After the fire, I called the president and told him our sad story of needing a place to go. That very week, he opened up an auditorium at a very affordable price.

Years later, after weathering several relocations, we had grown to be able to buy some property. We made a long wish list: on a major highway, a beautiful location, near a population hub, and more. We found a 20-acre spot that we could purchase for only $29,000 down. Our people sacrificed and came up with the money, and we were thrilled. Then we met with the local zoning board, and they absolutely refused to allow us to build a church facility. We took them to court, and we were still voted down.

God, where are you? we asked.

One day a lady called me and told me about her beautiful house. "We're moving, and my husband and I think a preacher should live there," she said. "We think that preacher should be you."

"I don't have any money," I replied.

"Just come look at it," she said.

We looked at it and loved it but still did not have any money. I went to bed praying about it and in my sleep came up with an idea. In the morning, I asked her if she would take a note— an IOU that we would pay in four years. She said yes, we moved in, and we were very happy.

As I drove away from the house each day, I kept seeing a certain tract of land along the freeway. It was on a lush, green hillside. It was directly across from a busy mall, which gave the property high visibility to thousands every day.

Who could dream of a better location?

God provided us a striking opportunity in the middle of adversity.

I inquired about who owned it. A little later I was a speaker at a banquet and found myself sitting next to the uncle of the property owner. I asked him to make an appointment with his nephew for me. He did.

God enabled our congregation to buy that property totally on options—on the promise that one day we would start paying for it, which we did. We sold the original 20-acre property and used the proceeds to help pay for a portion of the land we had on option and built our first multipurpose building.

God provided us a striking opportunity in the middle of adversity.

10. A Prevailing Faith Leader Endures

God encourages us to "run with perseverance the race marked out for us" (Heb. 12:1). By God's standards, every starter who endures is a winner. God's winners in Heb. 11 and 12 didn't give up the faith. They kept at it. They were steadfast and unmovable. They did what they could and counted on God to supply what they lacked. Because of their unwavering faith, they're listed in the Bible's "hall of fame."

We all know there are few guarantees in ministry. "We conquer by continuing," says George Matherson. And Josh Billings, American humorist of the 1800s, adds his advice: "Be like a postage stamp. Stick to one thing until you get there."

One of my Beeson Pastor Doctor of Ministry students won my heart when he said "Dale, I keep thinking of your earliest days at the drive-in theater, when you had to pick up the trash off the ground each week, sometimes the sound went out, sometimes it rained so hard that you and Margi almost got blown off the roof of the snack shack as you led."

Then he said, "I remembered that you stuck with the dream and didn't give up."

He discovered an important principle of ministry for all of us—never give up. Like the people listed in Hebrews, our inspiration was God. Many times I thought of Jesus' endurance. Scripture reports, "As the time drew near for his return to heaven, he moved steadily onward towards Jerusalem with an iron will" (Luke 9:51, TLB).

You, too, can achieve the greatest of dreams. Dedicate yourself and all your aspirations to Jesus Christ. He is the inspiration and the motivation of all worthy achievements. Heb. 12:3 points us to Jesus: "Consider him who endured such opposition from sinful men, so that you will not grow weary and lose heart."

I want to do something great for God with whatever life He has given me. I would rather attempt something great for God than to have material security, than to have the approval of people, than to fail to use what God has given me. I would rather attempt something great for God than to be bored with life. Let's do something great for God and build a faith-driven, prevailing church.

·2·

RISKY MISSION AT COMMUNITY CHURCH OF JOY
Safe and Sound or Dangerous and Exciting?
Walt Kallestad

A young lady phoned me and said, "Pastor Walt, I want to get married jumping off the side of a mountain. We'll rappel down the mountain, have the ceremony partway down, and then continue rappelling the mountain. Would you marry us?"

I replied, "Sure—I'll be happy to do that."

Then she told me that I had to practice. After I responded that I didn't think I would have time to learn mountaineering, she called back and said she had a team who would lower me down so that I could do the ceremony.

I would have no part of that. I wasn't going to be lowered down. I wanted to do the real thing—rappel a mountain. I made time to take a lesson.

When we got to the wedding, it was great. The press was there. They heard about the crazy minister who was going to be jumping off a mountain marrying people, so their photographers were below taking some nice shots, not all flattering to me. The story hit the front page of *Arizona Republic*, the primary newspaper in the area. It was a wild, crazy experience.

The woman who had asked me to preside over her wedding is a Harley-Davidson motorcycle rider. She said that as a gift for laying my life on the line to marry them, I could ride her Harley for a couple of weeks. I told her that would be fantastic—I'd love to do that.

I had such a great time on that motorcycle that the Harley bug bit me hard, creating a great deal of conversation between my wife and me. She finally agreed that I should go ahead and buy a motorcycle. So I bought a Harley and went to motorcycle school.

After going to class and getting my license, I took a ride out on the road and pulled up to a Starbuck's. As I got off the bike, a bunch of guys came over, looked at the bike, and said, "Hey, Harley Man—that's pretty cool. We're talking dirty. Why don't you come over to our table and sit and talk to us?"

I thanked them, got my coffee, and sat down with them. Sure enough, they were talking dirty. The conversation finally came around to who I was and where I worked. I wish you could have seen their faces when I told them I was a pastor at Community Church of Joy in Glendale, Arizona.

They stumbled around on their words and began mumbling. Then one of the guys said he didn't like Christians because they're a bunch of hypocrites. I asked him why he said that. He answered, "Ministers rip you off. Christians are gossipers. I know some who are doing bad things, even worse things than I do, and I'm not a Christian."

This conversation gave me an opportunity to invite them to check out the church I serve. I don't think they had received many invitations to church lately.

I've had many similar experiences like this. People don't expect a minister to climb down off a Harley. My hobby once opened a door for me to be a chaplain when more than a million bikers gathered in Sturgis, South Dakota. I saw this as a tremendous opportunity to reach out. One of the event organizers asked if I would bring a ministry team and lead in some worship. I agreed, although it was one of the most difficult ministry times of my life. I felt depleted, as if everything I could possibly give had been squeezed out of me. During that experience I learned a new definition of darkness.

I once read a book that included the story of an Episcopalian priest who went into a Honda shop to look for a motorcycle. When he began examining a Honda 750, a salesman came over and talked about the product. He told him about the speed, acceleration, and excitement. He drew attention to the attention-getting growl of the pipes, the racing capabilities, the sense of risk, and how all the good-looking girls would be attracted to anyone riding such a machine.

The priest then told the salesman that he was a minister. The salesman immediately changed his language and even the tone of his voice. He spoke quietly and told him about the good mileage, the visibility, and the practicality of such a machine.

This was the priest's conclusion: lawnmower salespeople aren't surprised to encounter clergy shopping for their merchandise, but motorcycle salespeople are. This tells us something about members of the clergy and about the church. Lawnmowers are slow, safe, sane, practical, and middle-class. Motorcycles are fast, dangerous, wild, and thrilling.

SAFE AND SOUND OR DANGEROUS AND EXCITING?

The question, then, is whether being a Christian is more like mowing a lawn or riding a motorcycle. Is the Christian life safe and sound, or is it dangerous and exciting? I'm afraid the common image of the Christian Church is pure lawnmower— slow, deliberate, and plodding. On the contrary, our task is to take the Church out onto the open road, give it the gas, and see what the old baby will do. This is what risk is all about. The essence of faith is risk.

Our task is to take the Church out onto the open road, give it the gas, and see what the old baby will do.

The movie *Apollo 13* shows a great space mission in which everything suddenly starts to go wrong. The simple statement "Houston, we have a problem" triggers a massive effort to rescue the mission. Much is at stake, especially human lives. The NASA leaders take huge risks at great personal costs, ultimately saving the astronauts and the spacecraft.

Leading sports champions seem to cultivate a life of risk. In recent years I was conducting some seminars in Europe and happened to end up at Saint Andrews and played the old course the last day before the Open. As I was coming down the 17th hole, I hit a picture-perfect drive and landed my ball right in the middle of the fairway. I mentioned to the caddy that I might be an emerging Tiger Woods.

"We don't like Tiger over here," he replied, explaining that he thought Tiger was just a hotshot, flash-in-the-pan player.

Many people, like that caddy, don't like risk-takers. But Tiger proved otherwise.

I was reading an article about Tiger Woods in the August 14, 2001, edition of *Time*. It explained how the best golfer in the world took a risk to become a much better golfer. When Tiger was champion of the Masters in Augusta, Georgia, he realized that he didn't have what it would take to be the best golfer in the world. So he did something about it. He risked it all. He went to school to relearn his swing. Many professional golfers who lay it on the line like that never come back. For 19 months Tiger didn't win a tournament. People were talking about how his former success wasn't for real. Meantime, he was working hard and risking it all to develop into a much better golfer.

Then he came back. The evidence—that there are now few who can beat him—shows that it was worth it. Tiger now holds most of the golfing records in the world today. Why was he willing to risk it all?

Mike Martz is the coach of the St. Louis Rams football team. He was the one who called the "hail Mary" pass to win the Super Bowl in 2000. He has a poem on his desk that says, "Give me courage, Lord, to take risks. Not the usual ones respected, necessarily relatively safe, but those I could avoid. The go-for-broke ones."

Our Biggest Risk at Community Church of Joy

In 1989 we were at a critical point in our ministry at Community Church of Joy. Our congregation had grown dramatically. We had a 14-acre campus. We began to look to the future after 100 drivers pulled away one Sunday after failing to find a place to park. I went to the board and told them we needed to find a new location. We brought in an expert, Lyle Schaller, to look at our situation and give us counsel. He told us, "This is the greatest risk you'll ever take. Your chances of failure are greater then your chances of success. It's like walking on a lake in northern Minnesota in the wintertime. There are places where the ice isn't frozen thick enough to walk on. You can easily fall through on the thin ice and possibly even lose your life. You have to make a decision. Do you want to risk it all? Do you want to lay it all on the line?"

We faced the realities of huge risk. When we took this risk, it turned out to be one of the most difficult periods in my personal life and ministry. My earliest years with the church pale in comparison to what we went through during our four years surrounding relocation.

You have to make a decision. Do you want to risk it all? Do you want to lay it all on the line?

But in 1998 we sold our old facility and moved to a new 200-acre campus. The costs of the move have been enormous financially, emotionally, and mentally. It had everything a great location should have—positioning along a major freeway, great visibility, and easy accessibility. However, when we relocated the new facility was not yet finished. We had no sidewalks or parking lots. For our very first days, we didn't even have power, so we had to rent generators. That was also the time El Niño hit. So it was raining and ugly, and many of our people asked why we had left our previous site. The old place was nice, and this one wasn't.

They decided the change was ridiculous, and 25 percent of our members left. It was devastating. When I first came to Community Church of Joy and started making changes the people didn't like, they had home meetings in order to get rid of me. Now, 20 years later, they were having home meetings again, once more to figure out how to get rid of this crazy Kallestad. The mail, E-mail, and phone calls devastated me. I could see that the staff was really struggling with this great risk, this great leap of faith we had taken.

In the midst of all of the transition, I went out for dinner with my wife, Mary. We were sitting at a traffic light, and I saw a car coming off the freeway. It was clear to me that the car wasn't going to stop at the light. Sure enough, it didn't. A utility truck was coming from the other way, and soon we witnessed a huge crash. The utility truck went flipping and turning. We heard sounds of glass shattering, crunching, and scraping. It was horrible.

Our mission statement is that all may know Jesus Christ and become empowered followers.

I grabbed my cell phone and called 911. Mary and I hopped out of the car and ran over to the truck, which had come to rest on the driver's side. As we approached it, a sandy-haired woman's head poked up. The lady's eyes were buggy as she looked around and said simply, "What was that?" She had glass all over her, but she told us she was not hurt. The other driver was all right as well.

I relayed this story to our staff and asked them if that wasn't somewhat how they felt. They could identify with that utility-truck driver!

Fortunately, over time we have grown by 40 percent again. Our target has never been trying to steal people from other congregations. We've never been in competition with churches around us. Our target audience is people who have never been connected with Jesus Christ or the Church. Our mission statement at Community Church of Joy is that all may know Jesus Christ and become empowered followers; we share His love with joy inspired by the Holy Spirit. That's our target.

RISK REQUIRES COMMITMENT FROM LEADERS

What are we willing to risk for people who are not connected to Jesus Christ or the Church? In the Bible we see some enormous risks and the reality that comes with risk. The apostle Paul writes in 2 Cor. 11:21, 23-28,

> I am speaking as a fool. . . . I have worked much harder, been in prison more frequently, been flogged more severely, and been exposed to death again and again. Five

times I received from the Jews the forty lashes minus one. Three times I was beaten with rods, once I was stoned, three times I was shipwrecked, I spent a night and a day in the open sea, I have been constantly on the move. I have been in danger from rivers, in danger from bandits, in danger from my own countrymen, in danger from Gentiles; in danger in the city, in danger in the country, in danger at sea; and in danger from false brothers. I have labored and toiled and have often gone without sleep; I have known hunger and thirst and have often gone without food; I have been cold and naked. Besides everything else, I face daily the pressure of my concern for all the churches.

Who do we think we are that as leaders we're going to get off scot-free? The greatest leader who ever walked the earth, Jesus Christ, ended up on a cross. Yet we struggle when there's pain and suffering. I will tell you this: the greater the risk, the greater the pain and suffering. As we look at people who are willing to lay it on the line, we know they've been through war. There are times we have to battle fatigue, tears, suffering, and enormous struggle. However, I must also tell you that the reality of risk, while dangerous and painful, also has a positive side.

RISK LEADS TO NEW DISCOVERIES AND NEW FRONTIERS

The importance of risk is that it brings new discoveries and new frontiers we can capture for our Master. There are also persons whose lives are transformed when we take risks. We discover some new and exciting ways to accomplish mission and ministry. One of the great pictures of the importance of risk is found in the movie *Patch Adams*. The medical student nicknamed Patch goes to the nearby hospital and entertains some children who are there for cancer treatment. The hospital administrator catches him, chews him out, and reminds him that the rules are there for a reason and that he must obey them.

But it's important to take risks in order to get out of the old box of tradition and the status quo. New discoveries in mission and ministry often come from people who are willing to risk and not simply conform.

God gives you permission to get out of the box. Dare to be different and experiment.

G od gives you permission to get out of the box. Dare to be different and experiment.

When I came to Community Church of Joy, we did some experimenting in areas of worship styles, organization, and programs to reach new people for Christ. We learned that the most important thing about risk is that we discover the extremities of God—that He has unbelievable capacity and that He is a immensely big God.

When we moved to our new church campus, we took a big risk financially. We moved from a $5 million campus to a $22 million campus. That was a stretch. We had to do a lot of trusting.

While going through this whole process, we were dealing with the financial struggle. We got a call from the bank saying that if we didn't have $2 million to them in two weeks, they would shut the project down. We gathered our leaders and trusted God. Then, a short time later, a banker called me from Sun City, Arizona, a suburb close to the church, to tell me that a certain 102-year-old lady had just died. We had never met her, but she had heard what Community Church of Joy was doing for children. "She loves children, so she left a gift for you," he explained. "She's left your church a gift of $2 million!"

That was God at work. Had we not risked, we would never have experienced that miracle gift. I could tell you many stories about God's provision. What God decides, He provides. I believe the importance of risk is that our faith is stretched. We have a beautiful campus, we continue to add new ministries, and it's an exciting place to be—but I tell people that is not what it is all about. Our people have had their hearts stretched by what we have been through. Their faith has grown. Our people are becoming more courageous and daring in their walk of faith. That's what it's all about. That's the bottom line importance of risk.

STRENGTH AND ENABLEMENT FOR TAKING RISKS

In 1 Thess. 5:17, the Bible tells us to never stop praying. In 1989, when we first started talking about this relocation project, I was working on my doctor of ministry studies through Fuller Theological Seminary. One afternoon when I came back from class, I sensed God calling me to spend time in prayer. So I put everything aside and started to pray. I had written a blueprint for what we developed. I believe God gave a very clear picture of what the plan was—the blueprint for our new mission center. But the key for it to become a reality was a solid foundation of prayer.

We must have a God-sized dream and believe that only God can carry it out.

I went back and told our decision group that we needed to take prayer more seriously. I firmly believed we should call a full-time pastor of prayer in order to do this. I remember one of the board members asking, "What is he going to do all day? Sit around and pray?" I let that hang in the air—and then said, "That's not such a bad idea!" The board eventually caught the vision, and we called a minister of prayer and built a prayer network. Our goal was to have over 2,000 intercessors by the year 2000, and we've exceeded that, along with prayer classes and prayer retreats. You have to get connected to God and stay connected to His heart through prayer. We must have a God-sized dream and believe that only God can carry it out.

One amazing reality for us as we were involved in this risky mission came one afternoon as the sun was setting. We located an orchard in a prime location where a new freeway was going to be located. As we deliberated relocating, I pled with God to let me know if this was important to Him—I didn't want to give my life to something that wasn't clearly in His will. I asked Him to shut it down and not allow us to go ahead if it was not His will. I drove to the back of the orchard and discovered a small trailer there. There was a car in front of it, so I decided to see who lived there.

An 80-year-old man with bibbed overalls and a stubby beard opened the door. I introduced myself and told him that I had been praying about whether God wanted us to buy this land and build a mission center there. He started to smile and invited me in. He introduced himself as Scotty and his wife as Ruthie. I sat down at the table with them. Ruthie had a big smile. I knew it wasn't a dangerous place, because they had a picture of Billy Graham on one wall and Jesus on the other. I felt pretty safe in this trailer with these strangers. The man asked me to tell his wife what I had told him, so I did. Then Ruthie started to cry. Then I saw Scotty's eyes get all watery and red. He apologized and explained that they had moved onto this land 40 years before. "Every night Ruthie and I hold hands, walk around this land, and pray that God would one day build a church here."

This sealed the confirmation in my heart. I decided I would be willing to risk it all for that. While I was still a little boy, God planted the seeds in this faithful couple who had prayed day after day for 40 years that God would do this. He was now answering their prayers.

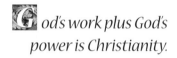 od's work plus God's
power is Christianity.

Ruthie died before we constructed our facility. Last year Scotty turned 90. He walks around our campus nearly every day. His eyesight is now very poor, and his health deteriorated to the point that he had to be placed in a nursing home. I saw him about a week ago at about eight o'clock at night. When he heard it was me, he literally jumped out of bed. To this day, he is still in awe of the power of prayer. And so am I.

Lloyd Ogilvie told me when I was a young minister that when it's our work plus our power, it's nothing more than humanism; God's work plus our power is simply religion; but God's work plus God's power is Christianity. If you want to do God's work with God's power, you always start with prayer.

Think of the results. 1 Cor. 2:9 says, "No eye has seen, no ear has heard, no mind has conceived what God has prepared for those who love him." When I see what has happened because of the risk that we took, I'm amazed. This past Sunday we had about 40 baptisms. We regularly have whole families baptized—families who tell us that they got involved in the school we were able to begin on our new property. First they came to the school and then decided to try the church. Now they don't want to miss a week. They tell me that their lives have been transformed.

We have a healing service one Sunday night each month. Every person who attends receives a paper with scriptures on them, which we read together. We anoint people with oil and pray for them. Amazing stories of transformed lives and healed hearts come from this time. I always leave that service thanking God for the privilege of being in ministry.

One couple in our church has started a ministry to the homeless in the inner city. The husband, Rob, quit a very successful career in advertising, selling out of the company to give his whole life to Missions of Mercy. One night Rob and his wife, Lisa, brought a prostitute to church. At the end of the service, she stood up and said curtly to Rob and Lisa, "You told them I was coming, didn't you?"

They said "No, we didn't tell them. Why?"

She replied, "You had to. He was talking to me the whole time. That's all he did. He just stood up there and talked directly to me." Rob and Lisa explained that it was the power of God using the Word of God to touch her life. The woman admitted then that she wanted her life to be different. She was a prostitute and was addicted to drugs. She explained to them that if she could stay clean for seven days, the Salvation Army had a program they promised she could go through to change her life. She went into the prayer room at the end of the service, and people prayed with her that she could stay clean for seven days. She did. Rob and Lisa told me they had received a phone call from her when she testified, "Rob and Lisa, you have no idea what it's like to be born again!"

What are we willing to risk so we can win people who are not today connected with Jesus Christ? Kent Hunter says that the United States is the third largest mission field in the world. Fewer people are going to church today than were attending 10 years ago, even as the percentage of population continues to grow. What are we willing to do to reach these lost people with the good news of Jesus Christ?

ARE YOU WILLING TO RISK IT ALL?

We have a woman named Linda in our church who has become very involved in the Angel Tree project. After she won an award for her work, a television crew come out and did a story on her. Last year she worked with our congregation, and we provided gifts for over 30,000 individuals.

Linda wasn't always able to function at that level of leadership. The first time we met was when she showed up on the doorstep around Thanksgiving. I was the only one around the church. She had two kids in the car. She told me that she had no money, no food, and no place to live and asked me what she should do. I told her our church could help. We helped determine what her needs were and provided food, housing, and money. She finally made it through that dark time and became successfully involved in real estate.

Now she shuts down her office from Thanksgiving to Christmas so she has time to minister to people during the holiday period. She gives to people in the name of Jesus. When she gives something, she always tells the reason why she's doing it.

There are so many other wonderful stories of transformed lives. Those victories are certainly worth the risk!

Once again I ask you: what you are willing to risk it all for? For what cause are you willing to lay everything on the line? For me, it's reaching lost people with the gospel. I'm committed to reaching those whose destiny right now is an eternity without Jesus Christ. I believe we must be willing to lead our churches to become tooled, equipped, empowered—to catch the vision for reaching out beyond ourselves.

It's the reality that leadership is all about risks.

Walt Disney at the Disneyland dedication said, "We did not build this for ourselves. We built it for others." If you're willing to build your faith communities and ministries for others, not being selfish but giving it away, God will honor you and your efforts. You'll then find that your best days in life and ministry are yet to be.

If I've learned anything during these 20-plus years I've been pastor at the Community Church of Joy, it's the reality that leadership is all about taking God-sized risks.

·3·

ARE WE DOING WHAT WE'RE SAYING?
Challenging Churches to
Go on Mission with Jesus
Bill Easum

Established churches in North America, once giants of innovation and passion, are now on the brink of boring irrelevance. In the short span of 50 years, many established churches in North America have gone from riches to rags. Systems theorists tell us that in times of great change, such as what our culture is experiencing now, many highly successful organizations fall on hard times. Very few "Fortune 500" companies of 1950 appear on that list today. A comparable turndown is at work in the Church—in both denominations and individual congregations. Several reasons can be given to explain the similarly rapid decline of established churches.

1. **Too many churches are declining because they've forgotten what business they're in.** They have lost their first love (Rev. 2:1-5) so they seem afraid to talk passionately about Jesus Christ. They're afraid of not being inclusive enough, or worse, of being bigots. As a result, they say little or nothing about Jesus, and the fire goes out in their hearts. They no longer see themselves as existing to introduce people to Jesus Christ or to reach their geographic area in His name.

I'm convinced that the number-one issue facing Protestantism today, including a large percentage of local congregations, is Jesus' question "Who do you say that I am?" (Matt. 16:15, NKJV).

Without Jesus Christ and His radical claims on our lives

and our churches, it's easy to be content with shuffling the deck chairs on the *Titanic* or soothing our consciences by adhering to the "righteous remnant" theory that the smaller the church becomes, the more faithful it actually is. Without Jesus Christ, the congregations we lead are nothing more than clubs on the lookout for just enough new dues-paying members to help support their programs and hold on to their buildings—a survival mentality that keeps everything just like it is.

On the other hand, we must find ways to profess Jesus Christ as Lord. I find the Jesus focus in all churches that are growing spiritual giants.

2. Churches are declining because they've organized around their loss of passion for Jesus. Instead of organizing to spread the gospel, they organize to run the institution. In effect, they circle the wagons and focus on organizational correctness.

> *ealthy churches and denominations focus on transforming people and society.*

It's not unusual for key leaders to spend most, if not all, of their time working within the church's premises, attending committee meetings, and doing all sorts of good things that have no spiritual outcome. Too many church members find their sense of "belonging" in the building called the church instead of in the community of faith, which has almost nothing to do with buildings. Going to meetings, maintaining ineffective programs, and preserving church facilities is often the number-one rival to the first commandment: "'Love the Lord your God with all your heart and with all your soul and with all your strength and with all your mind'; and, 'Love your neighbor as yourself'" (Luke 10:27).

Healthy churches and denominations focus on transforming people and society, not on the well-being of the clergy or satisfaction of the laity. For example, for two centuries my denomination's unwritten goal was to "spread scriptural holiness throughout the land and to reform a nation." The only way my own denomination will return to effectiveness is if we organize once again to spread scriptural holiness and to reform a nation.

Effective churches integrate mission and their organization. Let's say the stated mission of Community Church is to "relationally and lovingly invite people to Jesus Christ, disciple those who respond, and send disciples out into the world to serve in the name of Jesus Christ." With this mission, Community Church could organize around the words "invite," "disciple," and "send." Then every phase of ministry in that church would revolve around the stated mission, including staffing, budgeting, ministries, volunteers, and evaluation.

Integration of mission and organization insures that ineffective ministries are phased out and intentionally dropped. Leaders, including paid staff and volunteers, are trained, evaluated, and may even be terminated on the basis of the church's mission. Core ministries that enhance the mission receive the primary share of the church's time, energy, and money.

For example, most churches setting out to start a contemporary worship service try to do so on a shoestring. Launching a new church or starting a new service is one of the primary, innovative ministries in which people of today can experience God. Yet those outreach efforts seldom receive the lion's share of the resources, including staff, priority, prayer, visibility, and money. A large church's leaders told me recently they did not have funds to start a contemporary service the right way, so they were not going to do it. In the next breath they mentioned the fact that they had spent $500,000 remodeling the organ.

3. Churches are declining because they listen to and care more for their present members than for spiritually needy people outside the church. Like many successful organizations, many churches base what they're going to do in the future on what their present members want.

Let's apply that idea from secular organizations and the world of business to the Church. Many older church members aren't thrilled with contemporary music, so it gets rejected even though it would reach many more contemporary people than their classical service music. This reality shows in hundreds of other ways, too, like church service schedules, programming, and even the design and appearance of facilities. I know a good way to overcome this problem: When church committees discuss what new ministries to begin, they could get opinions from people in their target age-group *who are not attending any church.*

Providing only the services and ministry wanted by members is not a problem unless the world experiences a severe shift in new generations' attitudes and needs. And that's exactly what's happening now. Quantum changes are occurring in the way people perceive and experience truth. As a result, persons born before 1965 are not likely to have a good understanding of the needs of unchurched or pre-Christian people born after 1965.

We must keep one thing clear: Mission and core values do not change. At the same time, vehicles to get the mission accomplished do change, and strategies for communicating values need innovation in every generation. Methods change, but mission is changeless.

For example, the type of music that conveys the gospel today is much different from the music that communicated the gospel in the past. Our business is to share the gospel, not fight about church music. Church music is good music if it conveys the gospel and bad music if it doesn't convey the gospel. The mission does not change, but the type of music might.

On the contrary, the music tastes of leaders, including those who direct music and minister to youth, are not the determining factor; too many worship wars are nothing more than a selfish tenacity to have one's own way. The ruling question in this day of change must be "What does God want from me in this place at this time." His will is supreme, and mine must always be subordinated to His.

It's time we integrated our mission with the way we make decisions and carry out our lives as the Body of Christ. It's time to do what we say we believe. The churches that do will discover that the younger generations are just as willing to become a part of the Body of Christ as any other generation, just as willing to serve in the name of Jesus, and equally good stewards of all they have as any other generation before them.

4. **Churches are declining because too many church members have too small a vision of what it means to be part of the**

Body of Christ. As a result of not enough love for Jesus, church members place too much of their faith in "their" buildings and ask "their" pastor to be "their" personal chaplain. *They serve the institutional church more than the living Christ.* The good news of the gospel becomes "their" private property, with the church, the pastor, and the programs of the church existing primarily for them. The idea of "for the sake of the gospel" is at the heart of overcoming church members' resistance to change. It's time that we name it and take the heat.

When church members refer to "their" church, any encroachment on "their" territory is met with resistance. Otherwise, why would church leaders of dying churches become angry when their denomination plants a new church in close proximity to them in the hope of reaching the people not being reached by such churches? If spreading the gospel were their goal, what difference would it make if another church began ministry in "their" territory? The sake of the gospel is at the heart of overcoming church members' resistance to change.

Christians have a remarkably poor history dealing with change, even for the sake of the gospel. It's been my experience that when people are deeply in love with Jesus Christ, their longing for others to experience such love overcomes a multitude of fears. When people reach this level of spiritual maturity, they don't resist change if the change helps spread the gospel. Like Paul, they're willing to become all things to all people so that "they might win some." Christians have no choice in the matter. It's in their "DNA."

Every church I have ever worked with is filled with wonderful people. Some of these are so good that they would rather be nice than Christian when it comes to a taking on the bullies that try to hold back change. Many of these good people love the Lord so deeply that they're willing to risk failure "for the sake of the gospel." What they really need is a leader or board who refuses to play "pastor fetch" and who will nurture them, equip them, and help them find God's passion for their life. When they do, all resistance to change melts away "for the sake of the gospel."

INCREASE PASSION TO LOWER RESISTANCE TO CHANGE

How, then, do pastors help church leaders overcome their resistance to change? Certainly not by buying into the dysfunctional wisdom of many Protestant leaders, that pastors should spend the first year or two getting to know the people so that they will know where and how to lead them. Such wisdom assumes that church members want to go somewhere. In reality, most haven't given it any thought. And they won't think about it until a leader pushes the issue. The following are some ideas to help you get started bringing the church's way of doing her work into sync with her mission and vision.

Cultivate the Jesus view of people. Our Lord understood people, so He called them sheep. Sheep never go anywhere in particular; they just follow the easiest path of grazing. Many lay leaders have no idea of what the church is supposed to do or be. For that reason, they tend to want the church to be a supportive social organization—nothing much more—until they have some crises need in their lives.

Help people overcome their fear of change. Often resistance to change is simply fear. Fear of the unknown. Fear of the cost. Fear of losing some comfort. Fear of losing what they have. Fear of being out of control.

Only one thing is necessary to overcome resistance to change: church leaders have to want it badly enough to find a way. If the passion is great enough, they'll discover how to overcome people's fear of change.

Here's a personal example. When I felt the call to consult with churches nine years ago, I found that long, repeated travel was often necessary. However, I had a tremendous fear of flying—I had been on a plane only twice in my life. I found myself taking tranquilizers just to get on an airplane. I would sit there white-knuckled, flinching at every bump in the air. I arrived worn out and unable to give my best. I had to do something. I knew consulting was where God was leading me for the rest of my life, but how could I do it?

I searched for an answer, and a friend suggested that I learn to fly. A year later I got my pilot's license. Although I never became a great pilot, I fell in love with flying and overcame my fear. I now fly on commercial aircraft more than 100,000 miles a year. My last three books were written on an airplane, and just this year I fell asleep on a commercial flight for the first time.

What drove me to take flying lessons and overcome my fear? I simply could not live without doing so. The call to share with other churches what I was learning was too great. The same will be true for any leader. If your call to bring about change is great enough, you'll find a way to bring about that change.

Seek God's vision for your present assignment. Leaders have to sense God's passion for the work of God in a given situation and be willing to follow that passion. Change for the sake of change is not the goal. Leaders must have a vision of the future so strong that they can't exist without fulfilling it. Call it what you like, but they sense that it's God's will for their lives. They're willing to risk most of what they are and have in the hope of finding their place in God's world. The one thing they won't risk is not doing what they feel is God's will. They even risk the audacity and ridicule of thinking they know God's will. Church leaders have to be consumed by such a passion to bring about change.

Cultivate a sense of mission. Church leaders, it's time to find God's passion for your life and ministry. Stop being busy long enough to listen to what God wants from you. Take time out if necessary. Go off into the wilderness if necessary. Tell the church to cancel all of the business meetings for the next six months, and gather simply for prayer.

Do whatever you have to do, but get a vision for your assignment. Vision is what causes church leaders to accept change.

Now a word of caution: A vision is not an idea or new program. Vision has nothing to do with restructuring. Rather, it's something for which you are willing to lose almost everything in order to put it into motion.

Communicate passion. Passion for the work of the Lord is infectious. When the leader cares deeply about the will of God for a given assignment, the people will begin to care too—not with the same intensity as the leader, but they will move up and become a significant part of fulfilling that passion. Therefore, when you find God's passion for your church's ministry in your community and the world—

- Preach it over and over again.
- Talk about it everywhere you go.
- Bring it to every text you preach.
- Write it on your forehead.
- Recite it when you get up in the morning.
- Recite it when you lie down at night.
- Gather a group of disciples to pray about it.
- Live this way of life enthusiastically.

Being a leader who makes disciples is risky business in today's environment. Ask God for strength and focus on the Great Commission. Neither will ever fail you.

SPECIFIC STRATEGIES FOR INTEGRATING MISSION AND ORGANIZATION

Consider taking the following steps to be sure your church is driven by passion and vision.

Step 1: Develop a mission or purpose statement of no more than one short sentence.

Step 2: Decide on the church's core values that you feel are absolutely essential to being part of the Church.

Step 3: Reorganize, provide staffing, and budget around the mission or purpose statement. E-mail, the Internet, web page creation, and networking will be fundamental.

Step 4: Develop self-organizing, self-governing, self-ending teams based on clearly defined ministries arising from the mission or purpose statement. Accountability, not control, must be the organization's hallmark.

Step 5: Seek to develop partnerships or alliances with groups of any denomination with similar missionary objectives.

Step 6: Acquire and/or equip flexible, innovative, risk-taking, visionary leaders.

This chapter was adapted from Bill Easum's articles in Net Results, *a monthly journal of "New Ideas in Church Vitality." Bill Easum is president of Easum, Bandy & Associates. He may be reached at easum@easumbandy.com.*

4

MINIMIZING THE DOWNSIDE OF RISK
Recruiting and Developing the Right Staff

Leith Anderson

When I was first assigned the topic of this chapter, I wondered if I was the right person to deal with it. I wasn't sure if an outsider looking at the staff of Wooddale Church, where I have served since 1977, would necessarily list us as a group of risk-takers. Then I began to think about some of the risks we've taken: decisions like selling our building and moving nine miles across three towns, or changing the name of the church and its constitution and governance. We've also started new churches for other denominations, spent a lot of money on missions, and grown to six or seven weekend worship services. We also invite unbelievers to be creatively involved in ministry as a means of evangelism, such as when we sponsored debates with atheists and Christian scholars; hosted Muslims, Hindus, Buddhists, and Jews to come and present their best case in comparison to Christianity—all as a means of outreach.

Looking back at these events, I thought, "I guess these *are* risky things to do!"

All the risks we have taken are a part of a bigger process. This process hedges the downside of risk-taking and increases the predictability of success. The most important part of this is what we call prerisk management. It centers on our staff selection and church culture.

MINIMIZING RISK IN STAFF SELECTION

For us, about half of the pastoral staff is "home grown" from the church. About half, myself included, were not previously part of the church before coming to pastoral positions there. For us, the process of selecting staff is a significant part of having effectiveness and the ability to do some of the things that otherwise might be difficult to do effectively.

Identify the assignment

Typically, we will first decide what the position might be. If it's a vacant position, we'll decide if we want to fill it or change it to something else. Then we form a committee to work together to research and find a new staff person. That group typically will meet for weeks, sometimes months, to set up the processes and procedures before we actually go about the search. A very common procedure in many churches is to get right to the task and consider candidates before figuring out how to deal with those who are selected. Instead, we work on letters that will be sent, reference forms, the questions we're going to ask potential candidates.

Develop prospect list

At the same time, we seek to develop a lengthy list of potential candidates to fill a position. The typical way to do this is to put together a list of people who might know others in their area who would be suitable for this position. We would typically send out 100 letters to individuals who would know people in other parts of the country and ask them who they know they would recommend to us. With that letter, we put a couple of nomination forms and stamped, self-addressed envelopes in the packet. We also say that if we don't hear from them in two weeks, we'll have someone from the committee call to get their suggestion over the phone. Most of these people don't want a call, so they do return the forms even if they write on them, "I can't think of anybody, so please don't call." We also do advertising, both traditional and online.

Work on culling the list

Then the names start to flow in, and we set up a notebook and assign numbers to each candidate for all information that comes in on him or her. Then, unless there's an obvious reason to exclude the candidate, one member of the task force is assigned to him or her, and that member does some research before the candidate is contacted. We then conduct 15- to 20-minute interviews with at least three to five of the references, if available, for each candidate and include that information in the notebook. If we have only a name and background and no references on the person, it's not hard to think of another pastor or church in that part of the country and to call for possible references. We choose never to go inside the church or ministry where the person is currently functioning.

Ninety percent of the potential candidates are eliminated as we work through these processes. We then have two to six good candidates left. At that point, a carefully written letter with my signature goes to each candidate. It includes features that identify it as a very different kind of letter. For example, it's never a metered letter but instead includes a commemorative postage stamp. Instead of using 12-point type on the envelope, we use 14-point. Instead of a white envelope, we use ivory. We want it to look a bit different from the rest of the mail the person regularly receives .

Follow-up processes

The letter simply says that our church is looking for a pastor for young adults and that the candidate has been highly recommended to us as someone who is qualified for the position. It continues by stating that I am going to give the person a call in the next few days to see if there would be a time that's mutually suitable in the next few weeks when I can come and visit with him or her for a day. I will then call the person in the next day or two so there's no time to write back and say he or she isn't interested. I then accommodate my schedule the best I can to fly to meet the person wherever he or she is located.

No questionnaires or further requests for information are sent to the candidate. We're doing everything we can to woo and win the person and treat him or her with respect. Part of that grows out of experiences with other churches who are seeking staff members.

Then someone else and I will go to that person's home for a day. I'll go with about 30 pages of questions, which usually takes from 6 to 12 hours to go through. I cover a wide array of questions, from spiritual life to doctrine to practice in ministry. After that's over and my notes are written up back home, I have the search team ask me questions about the individual. If it's decided that this person is not the right person for the ministry position, we say thank you and pursue others.

Invite prospects to visit

If we decide this is someone we're interested in, we invite him or her to come to Minnesota to check out Wooddale Church. Then we check out some further things about the candidate. We've already asked his or her permission to do a credit check. We ask the candidate to take a drug test. We ask for transcripts from schools attended. We also ask the person to spend a half-day with an industrial psychologist, who tests and evaluates him or her. A second trip includes visiting with the pastoral staff and other people, depending on the specialized ministry that person might be involved in. The last trip would include a visit with the elder board and pastoral staff and an offer of the position.

It's well worth the work to be thorough in the front-end process.

Is this process a lot of work? Yes. Is it expensive? Yes— plane tickets cost hundreds of dollars. Does it take my time? Absolutely.

The other alternative, though, is to get the wrong person. That's even more expensive. It takes severance pay and months to transition someone out. You do damage to that person and others within the life of the church. Then you spend time and money recruiting someone else for the position. Therefore, it's well worth the work to be thorough in the front-end process.

It is a little like dating. The more experiences you have, the more thorough you are, the better it is for everyone involved. For us, that typically means it usually takes 6 to 12 months. We've actually taken as long as two and a half years. We were looking for a business administrator and were getting nowhere. We finally ran an ad in the *Wall Street Journal* and received around 1,000 applications. It took a while to process that many applications. We finally ended up with someone who was wonderfully qualified and now is in his seventh year with us.

DEVELOPING CORPORATE CULTURE THROUGH STAFF DEVELOPMENT

You may be thinking, *How does corporate culture relate to risk-taking?* Let me explain. I believe the development of our corporate culture is an essential foundation for taking calculated risks. So getting the right person is the beginning of the process, but then the person must be shown how he or she fits in the whole picture.

Staff supervision is also important. In our system, everyone reports to one person—never to a committee or to two people. We require written staff reports to that supervisor. We also require annual goals and written reports. In our system, I'm the only one who reports to a group because as a senior pastor I report to the board of elders.

Selection and personal growth

We recruit staff. We supervise them and develop them. New staff members attend our leadership training to understand how the church works. They are required to read certain books and do assignments. They must have annual goals as part of their development.

We require in-service training. If someone is from the life of the church and does not have theological training, we require that. We pay for it and give him or her the time off. We require the person to at least complete a master's level, but often it is through a doctoral level.

We also give staff members an opportunity to change positions on the staff. For example, Ken Geis was our singles pastor and transitioned to outreach pastor and from outreach pastor to executive pastor. In fact, most of our staff have had more than one position, because they develop and change. We continually ask, "How can we develop you as a person in a way that's in the best interest of the ministry of Wooddale Church?

Regular staff meetings

An important part of staff development is staff meetings. We require all staff to meet together twice a day, five days a week. We meet at 10:00 every morning and 3:00 every afternoon. It's an informal coffee break time, but everyone is required to be there unless he or she has someone in the office or has some other good reason not to attend. These meetings include pastoral and support staff.

The hub for us is at 8:00 every Monday morning when the pastoral staff meets together. No one takes Monday off. It seems to me that if you're going to be tired and depressed and suicidal, you should be paid for that day! We do some reflecting on the past weekend—some but not much. We mostly look ahead.

Written reports

Every pastor is asked to have a written report that is submitted by each Friday. These reports are stapled to other reports. For example, for each visitor who attended the previous weekend, we get a printout that lists the name, address, and how that person came to our church. We also include a customized follow-up for every single person who has visited the previous weekend. All reports become a 50- to 60-page booklet that everyone receives before the Monday morning staff meeting.

> *I think the church should be the leader of the business and civic community.*

Sometimes we talk about nitty-gritty, mundane, everyday issues, and sometimes we discuss broad and significant concepts. We ask that any person who has asked for any ministry in the church must first have his or her named cleared on Monday morning. You can't ask someone to usher, sing, or work in the nursery until first you've cleared that name with the pastoral staff. We ask the pastoral staff to list the names of everyone with whom they have met or had a significant telephone conversation within the past week. That way we are supervising each other as well as protecting ourselves from the person who will take three hours each week from each of us, which becomes the same as having the equivalent of a full-time employee just working for one individual. In addition, we have a staff chapel each Monday morning that is part of the staff meeting.

A bank officer in our community once asked if he could come to our Monday morning staff meeting. He came, and then I ran into him at the end of the day. I asked him what he thought. He answered, "I wish—how I wish—we could get all the managers of our bank to come to one of the Monday-morning meetings to see how an organization is run right." I think that's the way it ought to be. I think the church should be the leader of the business and civic community. If we're doing God's work, we ought to be doing as well or better than they're doing other work.

Sharing common experiences

We share common experiences. It's important for the staff of the church to have experiences they share. For the pastoral staff, we do one-day retreats about every two months. In the beginning of the year, we go overnight and take family to a retreat center. We have no agenda—we just hang out and swim. Our children are there. We do another each year in which we go and visit other churches. Another retreat is a time where we just pray together. One time we went to a monastery and just prayed together and individually for the day.

At other times we spend time planning or doing in-service training. Sometimes it's just an experience together. At least once a year we take a day just for an experience. Once we went to the county jail; we were all fingerprinted, photographed, and put in cells. That was a unique experience! One time we went to the Mayo Clinic and all watched surgery together. Another time we went inside a gutted 747 airplane and watched it being rebuilt. We met with the senior editorial staff of the area newspaper once. They told us that in all of their journalistic careers, they had never met with a group of pastors before. It was interesting, because pastors can often be critical of journalists, but they don't know them or reach out to get to know them. One of our experiences included visiting a Mormon chapel, a Muslim mosque, the Temple of Eck (which is a world-wide religion with its headquarters in our area), and a Kingdom Hall of the Jehovah's Witnesses. It's a lot more fun to go to their place than have them come to your house!

We did all this and then processed it all together. This is all part of this team-building function.

Written polices

I'll admit that at Wooddale Church we have plenty of policies. Sometimes they're for legal reasons. We have a computer policy, a sexual harassment policy, a vacation policy, and so on. Every year staff members have to sign a statement that they've read all of the policies and that they'll abide by them.

However, the larger the staff and the larger an organization, the harder it is to manage by rules and policy. It becomes more important to manage by corporate culture. Rules can only tell you what to do about what has happened in the past or what one person can anticipate for the future. Corporate culture can tell you what to do in the previously unanticipated.

▪5▪

RISKING A CULTURE OF CREATIVITY
Creativity, Efficiency, and Effectiveness
Leith Anderson

Every church needs creativity, imagination, and informed intuition. One management specialist calls creativity "breakthrough thinking."

New ways of thinking and doing must be steeped in a thorough understanding of the faith and tied to a savvy perception of current trends. In order to practice breakthrough thinking for our time, it's well to remember that many advances throughout Christian history were at first thought absurd or preposterous. That's why we work to see that creativity permeates the corporate culture of our church. Our God is the Creator of creativity, originality, and fervor. And He is often up to something very new.

A culture of creativity means we ask staff and lay leaders to come up with new ideas that are culturally appropriate. A great idea for Lexington, Kentucky, does not necessarily fit well in the Twin Cities of Minnesota. We want creative ideas that will work in our setting.

CREATING A CULTURE OF CREATIVITY

If we expect creativity, we have to give people permission to fail. Here's an example: as an outreach event, we invited top-flight representatives of the world's major religions—Buddhism, Hinduism, Judaism, Islam, and Christianity—to speak to us. The place was packed with thousands of people. Representatives had equal time to present their best case. It was a great idea that didn't work for us. The Christian had a plane delay and arrived after the event was over. It was not one of our great successes!

Ten minutes after it was over, a group of us huddled and asked ourselves what we were going to do next. What would our next creative venture be? We were not willing to allow the present difficulty to squelch creativity for the future.

Creative ideas that have come from our staff include events like conducting a church service as part of the grand opening of the Mall of America, one of the largest tourist destinations in the United States. Our grand opening event became front-page news in the *Minneapolis Star Tribune* and appeared in wire services and newspapers all over the country. It was a staff idea that required taking a risk.

Community use of facilities is another creative risk. We rarely allow other Christian groups to use our facilities, but thousands of people come every week from area businesses to conduct their staff meetings in our building.

Another creative staff idea that was borrowed from somebody else concerned Christmas Eve. Christmas Eve is a big deal in Minnesota, and churches have terrific attendance. Someone suggested we do an early Christmas Eve service around the 20th or 21st. It seemed like a goofy idea, but we decided we would try it one year.

We decided that we would deem this event a success if 150 people showed up. *One thousand* people showed up! An interesting thing happened. The Minneapolis newspaper typically runs two front-page religion stories per year, on Christmas Eve and on Easter. On Christmas Eve in past years they naturally could never run a photo of a church service, but they could that year because they could have one of our early Christmas Eve service and still meet their deadline. We try to continually encourage that type of creativity.

Efficiency has high priority

Efficiency is another important part of the corporate culture. We're witnessing an epidemic of excellence today. People expect excellence from their vehicles, hotels, telephone service —just about everything. Therefore, they expect it in the church too. For us that includes a real person answering our phone. You don't get a voice mail system when you call our church. This type of effort involves a disciplined use of money and running the church as an efficient business. It involves expecting hard work and expecting people to produce.

Effectiveness is more than efficiency

In his book *The Effective Executive* Peter Drucker writes, "Efficiency is doing things right. Effectiveness is doing the right thing." He's right on target. You can do the wrong things well, and you can to the right things poorly. What we want is both efficiency and effectiveness. For us that means excellence. We're doing the right things and doing them well. In addition, we constantly measure to find out how we're doing. For instance, when people visit the church, a certain percentage of them are selected to give their feedback. In the business world, this would be parallel to a customer service evaluation. We ask such questions as "Were you greeted?" and "Did you find your way around the building?" Each week we read evaluations that come from these people.

Input from target populations

We're particularly bent toward outreach, so we want to know what unchurched people think about what we're doing. For example, we've actually recruited unbelievers to tell us what they think of what we're doing. Once we enlisted a group of unbelievers to come to any one of four Sunday morning services up to but not including Easter. Then we had them in a focus group behind one-way glass and asked them to critique the preaching and the service. Talk about threatening! I remember one man, a realtor, who said, "I'm an agnostic—I don't know what I believe. I liked that guy up front. I think he and I believe the same thing." The point here is that risk is taken within a cultural context of creativity, efficiency, effectiveness, and excellence.

DECIDING WHICH RISKS TO TAKE

There's a limit to how many risks we can take, and we want to get the right ones. If we choose the wrong risks, we may detract from what we should be doing. That would mean we would not get the right thing done because we were spending our time doing the wrong thing.

Another significant concern is that we might take the wrong risk and succeed at it. Sometimes you can do the wrong thing exceptionally well with enormous popularity. It then looks like success but is in fact failure.

That means we should ask some questions:

1. Does this fulfill the purpose of the church? Our purpose is to honor God by making more disciples for Jesus Christ. We must ask ourselves, *Does this risk accomplish that?* One of our definitions for "honor" comes from the Greek word *doxa,* from which we get our English word "doxology." This word is most often translated *glory* or *to glorify God.* I became interested because I found as I was growing up in the church, I routinely prayed and said, "This glorifies God" and "That glorifies God," and I had no idea what the word meant. I did some research and discovered in the etymology of the word *doxa* that one of the root meanings had to do with reputation, especially enhancing reputation.

Therefore, to glorify God is to enhance God's reputation. Another way to think about this is that God and who He is cannot be improved upon; however, His reputation often doesn't line up with His greatness. Therefore, what we're called to do is bring God's reputation into alignment with who He truly is. The question that we're continually asking, then, is "If we take this risk, will it fulfill the purpose of the church, and will it enhance God's reputation in this particular context?"

Officials of a local Christian school, which encompassed kindergarten through 12th grade, approached us about taking over and running it. It was ours for the taking. We said no. Another time we were offered a radio station. We turned it down. We were offered a camp, and we said no to that as well. We frequently get requests for concerts, lectures, and conferences. We frequently find ourselves saying no because they don't fulfill our purpose.

2. Do we have the appropriate resources? Do we have the time, people, and money in order to do this right? We have had some situations in which we have started things and then just did not have resources to sustain them. We now have a very viable and effective Saturday evening service, but when we first started doing it, we just did not have a "critical mass." It was a different style of worship from Sunday morning, and it was consuming us. We had to shut it down because we realized that we didn't have the resources required to sustain it in the way it needed to be done correctly.

3. What is the predictability of success? What are the chances that this risk is actually going to work? The other side of the question is "What if it works really well?" We decided we would start a new church just down the road from us. The other churches we had parented were in more distant cities. We decided the senior pastor of this new congregation would be Joel Johnson, a wonderful guy with a winsome personality and a beautiful family. He had been on the staff of our church for 15 years. We launched the church with three services and 850 people the first Sunday. By one measure, that was a huge success. It raised the question of the predictability of how it would affect the life of Wooddale Church.

4. What are the probabilities or consequences? In systems theory, if you change one part of the organization, you change all parts of the organization. If the risk is to add another service, what is that going to do to Sunday School, parking, and everything else? If the question is adding a new building, what is raising that amount of money going to do to the general fund of the church, the missions giving, and the ability to recruit and support additional staff? What is going to happen to other giving? If we start new churches, what happens to our church if many of our people leave and go to that new church? All these are questions we want to ask in the process of choosing the risks we're preparing to take.

I don't want to give the impression that we're so thorough as to do all these things sequentially. However, when this is the general approach to risk-taking, we minimize the downside and maximize the upside. Specifically, we go through what we need to do to be ready, get set, and actually go for it.

5. What research is available? We find that people come up with terrific, clever ideas that we think have never been tried before. A couple of hours on the phone calling around the country shows us that there are at least a dozen other churches that have successfully or unsuccessfully done what we think is this original idea. We try to find every piece of information available.

We find out who else has tried this and, if need be, go see them and find out what lessons there are to be learned. That will save us a lot of trouble, mistakes, and money.

For example, Wooddale Church decided to relocate. In terms of research, we had a couple of people who spent a couple of days on the phone. This was not a huge task. They called all over the United States to find examples of churches that had relocated in the past five years. We came up with 50 examples. We asked some volunteers to do longer interviews and as many of these churches as possible to send literature to us. Out of that, we narrowed the 50 churches down to 12. Then a team of us went around the country and visited those 12 churches. We learned millions of dollars' worth of great ideas as we asked similar questions to all of them.

One of the questions regarded what they would do differently if they had it to do over again. Of the dozen churches we visited, the answers were all different except for one. All 12 said they didn't buy enough land. Whether the church had bought 5 or 150 acres, every one of them said they didn't buy enough land. At that point we had already spent most of our money on a piece of land, but we went back and used all our available financial resources for the purchase of more land. We didn't have any money left to construct a building at that time, but if we hadn't made that decision then, Wooddale Church wouldn't be nearly as large or effective as it is now. We learned that lesson from those 12 churches.

We also learned some very ordinary lessons. One of the major complaints in church buildings is that there aren't enough rest rooms. In our trips around the country, we discovered something we had never known. A church had done a survey and discovered that a large percent, something like 80 or 85 percent, of the ladies who go into a rest room go in for the purpose of looking in the mirror. This is especially true in a northern winter climate where people are coming in from snow, wind, or rain. What that church had chosen to do was put eight-foot mirrors in the hallways near the entrances. The mirrors cost a few hundred dollars and saved 50,000 dollars in building larger rest rooms. We never would have figured that out by ourselves.

We decided we were going to go to a Saturday evening service and asked ourselves what time it should begin. We did some research by calling every church we could find throughout the greater metropolitan St. Paul and Minneapolis area that had Saturday night services and asked them what time they started. Ninety-six percent of these were Roman Catholic churches, and almost all of them started their Saturday services around five o'clock. I concluded that their judgment was wrong, that five o'clock was too early, so we went with six o'clock. What we discovered was that many of the people we were trying to reach wanted to go out to dinner or to other events, and if the service was from six to seven o'clock, they couldn't get into restaurants easily, and other events had already started. Therefore, our starting time eliminated the very audience we were trying to reach; the Catholics were right. The point is that research had already been done, and we should have been wise enough to follow it.

Research like this is not difficult to get and is virtually free; it just takes some work to discover. Our staff talks about the research and moves on to planning, which is a written proposal for whatever is the risk that we're going to take. On that paper we say that this particular undertaking has this purpose, these resources, this budget; these are the dates we're going to attempt it; and this is the person responsible. Then the staff sits down and reviews the proposal and changes it as needed for it to be an effective instrument in getting the plan accomplished. For example, when we changed our Sunday morning program to go to five services and three Sunday School hours, the complexity of that gave me headaches. The services had to start at times that fed into the Sunday Schools, and we couldn't have children's Sunday School classes that started after the services began. We also had to figure out how to handle the complexities of parking. Our staff went to a hotel and spent one day from eight in the morning until five in the afternoon with white boards to try to find different ways to the right plan. We were risking the possibility that by changing the Sunday morning schedule, the whole thing would crumble down on us. Figuring out that plan was crucial.

6. **Why not run a trial project without making a permanent commitment?** One of the more common questions I'm

asked by church leaders is "What if we go to a second or third service and it doesn't work? Some people are opposed to it. I don't know if the church nursery workers and choir members will go along with it." Generally, I propose that for the four Sundays up to and including Easter, they try the number of services they want, then discontinue the plan and take the summer to evaluate it; and then, if it's a successful experience, begin the multiple services again. If it doesn't work, the church can just go back to the way it was before. What happens is that most people who say they're against it will be willing to live with it for four weeks. After you've done it, they can see what it looks like and are much more amenable to the whole idea. Prototype is a powerful tool for effecting that kind of change. If it's successful, you continue it; if not, you declare it a success and discontinue it.

We don't want to lose the younger generation of the Church.

For us, one current challenge we're facing is how to reach people who are drawn to a liturgical style of church service. Currently we have six weekend services at Wooddale Church. We have one Saturday night service and five Sunday morning services. Two of them are traditional services, and four are contemporary services. The traditional services have a robed choir, the Lord's Prayer, the Apostle's Creed, hymns, an orchestra, and one of the largest pipe organs in the United States. The contemporary services have casual dress, drums, drama, synthesizers, worship choruses, and all the things typically associated with contemporary worship. What we're currently deliberating is how to reach people who are from traditions in our area who appreciate the history of the liturgy and want liturgical worship. We also have a concern about younger adults in their 20s. The contemporary worship experience may be primarily a baby boomer phenomenon. We're finding many of the younger adults don't like it and desire something much more traditional. We don't want to lose the younger generation of the Church. Currently we're experimenting with liturgical worship for that generation.

WHAT ABOUT POLITICAL IMPLICATIONS OF CREATIVITY?

Along the way, there will always be politics. The Greek word *polis* means "city" or "the way things work." "Politics" is not a bad word—it's just the way things work. In any church in any community are constituencies. What we need to do is consider how the risk we're going to take affects these various constituencies. We need to make decisions that will engage the informal organization. There's a difference between the formal and informal organization. The informal organization should always decide first.

I have officiated at many weddings at Wooddale Church. If a couple want to get married, they meet with a pastor and participate in premarital seminars. All the issues are discussed before the wedding is approved and goes onto the calendar. Then we get to the actual rehearsal. If I'm conducting the wedding, I have the couple come down the aisle, and then I ask them some questions. I use the same jokes at every rehearsal, because ideally they are different people every time. I tell them that the answer to all the questions is yes. Then we practice giving the rings. Invariably the guy goes for the wrong ring. There must be some principle there that he naturally goes for the ring he's going to wear and not the ring he's supposed to give. Anyway, we go through all this stuff down to the detail. The next day at the wedding, everything goes smoothly. I've never had a father say he didn't know who was going to give the bride or a couple refuse to take their vows. The reason is that the wedding is the formal organization's ratification of the informal organization's decision.

The same thing is true in the life of the church. It isn't the vote in the business meeting, but it is the informal decisions that are made before that. Does it take a lot of work? Indeed it does. It is not the pledges that are made in the underwriting of the budget; it is the preparation that is done earlier. It is the informal organization. Politics means we work the informal organization to get ownership. If there's not going to be ownership, then we back down and don't do it. That reduces the chances of failure with risks.

Are there risks we're not willing to take? Yes, there are, and sometimes politics is a part of the reason. Here's an example. We had a request from a Muslim group who wanted to use one of our rooms every Friday for prayers. In the pastoral staff meeting, we discussed how we should respond to this. Our missions pastor said, "This is a great idea because we'll going to get to know Muslims, to be able to befriend them. They'll get familiar with our facility. We'll set up another prayer meeting in the next room and pray for them while they're praying." That was his logic. By the way, a mosque is an Islamic house of prayer—what they were asking to do was to set up a mosque in our facility. We are serious in our concern to reach people for Jesus Christ. However, our final decision was that this was a risk we are not willing to take. It would be very difficult to explain and would be so distracting from everything else we were doing that the potential benefits were not great enough to warrant it.

EXAMPLES OF RISKS TAKEN AT WOODDALE CHURCH

Starting new churches has been a major risk for us. In 1989 and 1990 we were in the process of building a new worship center, a very expensive endeavor. The final cost was three times the amount that any of us thought we were capable of. That meant taking on debt and all kinds of stretching for us. It was about that time that I went into a classroom at Bethel Seminary in St. Paul and saw something left over from a previous class. It was a piece of newsprint that said, "The most effective way to reach people today for Jesus is starting new churches." It stuck in my mind.

I returned and asked the staff and elders to hire a new church pastor and give that pastor unlimited recruiting rights within Wooddale to start a new daughter church that would open the same day we moved into our new worship center. The belief all the way around was that this was insanity. We needed every dollar and every person we could possibly get. Some thought that to give away hundreds of people to start a new church was foolish, and it would put the life of Wooddale Church at unnecessary risk.

Despite those reservations, we hired Paul Johnson, and he started Woodridge Church. It's now a congregation of over a thousand people and has itself started a daughter church. This success has led us to plant other new churches every two years or so.

More recently we took over a 150-year-old church. We closed it down and reopened it with new people. We're constantly recruiting people out of Wooddale Church. That's a risky thing to do. But what we've discovered after 10 years of experience and many wonderful newly started churches is that *our attendance and offering do not reflect any of these departures.* When you graph it, you can't even tell when the people who started these other congregations left Wooddale Church.

We've discovered after 10 years of experience and many newly started churches that our attendance and offering do not reflect the statistics of the people we contributed to the starts.

Another risk was starting church plants for other denominations. At a conference of the International Bible Society in Colorado Springs I shared my deep conviction that we need to be building the Kingdom and not just local congregations and denominations. Afterward, representatives of three denominations came to me and said that if I really believed that, they would like Wooddale Church to start a church for them. I decided to do it. The first venture was to start a Reformed church. We did some research, and to our knowledge, it was very possibly the first time a congregation had voluntarily started a church of another denomination. I know it's been done involuntarily many times, but we're talking voluntarily. We recruited a minister who came onto our staff and had almost a year to recruit people from our congregation, who then went out and started a Reformed church.

This past year we started a Southern Baptist church. Currently we're in contact with people of numerous other denominations with the goal of helping them be effective in reaching people for Jesus Christ in our community.

LESSONS FROM A WORLD CHAMPIONSHIP RISK

Back in 1991, the Minnesota Twins were in the World Series. It was the seventh game and the ninth inning of the series, and the score was close. Jack Morris was the pitcher for the Twins. He was already one of the oldest pitchers in the major leagues and had pitched more than eight innings of the game. He had been in far longer then he should have in any game, let alone the last inning of the last game of the World Series. Tom Kelly, the manager of the Twins, walked out to the mound, put his arm around him, and told him he had done a great job and that now they were going to put in a relief pitcher.

Jack replied, "T. K., I can do it. I know I have it in me. I can finish this game." The manager decided to leave him in, knowing that it was just a game. The Twins went on to win the 1991 World Series.

Did Tom Kelly take a risk? Yes, an enormous one—the World Series championship. Then again, I'm not so sure he did, because he knew his pitcher and knew his team. They had played together the entire season. Based on what he had previously known and previously done, he was willing to let Jack Morris finish the game. I think that's exactly the kind of approach that we as church leaders in the staff of our churches need to use as we approach the risks God has called us take.

∎6∎

PLANNING WORSHIP THE WAY WE'VE NEVER DONE IT BEFORE
Giving Worship to the People

Sally Morgenthaler

Worship happens every seven days in most churches, 52 weekends a year. Worship services take place whether we're ready or not, whether we're creative or not, whether we bring our full selves to the task or bring only what's left after everything else has taken priority. In a world that has become increasingly engaged with things spiritual, our worship services have more potential to impact people's relationships with God than ever.

The operative word, however, is "potential." Do third-millennial citizens really want the worship experiences we have to offer? In case you haven't noticed, there's a whole lot of competition beyond the church parking lot. Unlike the antispiritual climate of just two decades ago, the new millennium is a hyperspiritual era, fostering a seemingly endless supply of spiritual mutations and permutations. The result is a dizzying marketplace of world religions, offshoots, philosophical strains, and personal worldviews, combining and recombining at exponential rates and creating—in theory—as many faith options as there are inhabitants on the planet.

RISK REALITY

In the midst of such a kaleidoscope of faith options, the people who live at our doorstep are becoming increasingly adept at creating their own sacred space and experiences. From ad hoc, spray-painted shrines in the rubble of the World Trade Center to the Olympics' closing ceremony, "Prayers on Ice"; from Central Park candle vigils accompanied by Samuel Barber's *Adagio for Strings* to U2's opening "Hallelujah" chant at the Grammys, the world is worshiping without us and will continue to do so in ways we never could have imagined.

> *he world is worshiping without us and will continue to do so in ways we could never have imagined.*

We may cringe. But the spiritually engaged have now co-opted many of the expressions we in the Church once held as Sunday-exclusive: praise, prayers, rituals, laments, litanies, creeds—the list goes on. We may wax defensive, labeling such expressions as "isolated phenomena," worship knockoffs devoid of truth, and pop culture's misguided attempts at God connections.

Whatever our evaluation, we dismiss these new realities to our peril. Part mysticism, part spectacle—and with a genius that eludes even the most cutting edge in third millennial Christendom—a new worship species has quietly but ever so surely developed outside our walls. Here the planet's collective religious past is unapologetically plundered and rearticulated in a multisensory symphony of global art forms and technology.

A mélange of sophistication and simplicity, the new worship-without-church is not the future—it is here. Here, while we continue to squabble over hymns or praise choruses. Here, while the creative worship options in most congregations are still limited to singing and preaching. Here, while we keep trying to herd attendees into seeker or believer sections. Here, because the decidedly spiritual people beyond our gray walls could not wait for us to move on. Past our tightly held labels and categories to synthesis. Past our black-and-white compartments to Technicolor. Past the way we've always done it and into the now, where all time periods, geographies, tribes, ages, and styles are usable hues in the vast palette of God encounters.

Many of us as leaders have spent a great deal of time and

energy piecing together a view of the world that is manageable, that is, an environment we can mold by sheer authority and consistency. Surely, if the leadership paradigms we were taught 20 years ago are true—that being a leader is first and foremost about control—then a universe in disarray is not an option.

Ah, but that's exactly what we have: a universe in disarray, an age of profound uncontrollability and increasing discontinuity. Not long ago, a surprisingly short list of institutions controlled the dissemination of the world's information, shaping the educational, economic, political, and spiritual lives of millions. In the past two decades, the digital revolution has effectively eliminated the need for information hierarchies, bringing knowledge to quite ordinary people at the click of a mouse.

If we would carry God's kingdom into the hyperspiritual age—one that emerged to a great degree because of the breakdown in religious hierarchical structures—then as leaders we must recognize the futility of creating controllable, cocooned Christian worlds. We must stop building worship subcultures out of our own fear of change or fixation on the past, regardless of whether that past is 1955, 1985, or 1995. *True leadership engages the world as it exists in this moment. It risks reality.* What is reality when it comes to worship beyond the safe, gray box? The world is now spiritually self-initiating and, for the first time in history, ritually self-sufficient.

he world is now spiritually self-initiating and, for the first time in history, ritually self-sufficient.

Yes, it would be simpler if the Church still had the only corner on the divine marketplace, if people flooded our sanctuaries when they wanted to experience God in their lives. Yes, it would be easier if we could just scroll back to the days when there was a definable "outside" and "inside," a sacred and a profane, people and places that God inhabited, and people and places that God shunned.

But that world is long gone—by 50-some years. What's more, it's doubtful that it was even biblical. Check Acts 10—11 for how God broadened the definitions of "clean" and "unclean." The only thing we'll get by hanging onto it is a lack of effectiveness.

The first and greatest risk of effective ministry is to see things as they are, not as we wish or need them to be. Risk reality. Observe the intentionally unchurched at worship, and take note. Take lots of notes on what's happening outside the Church in the culture all around you.

For instance, the leadership team at a church in Bellingham, Washington, realized that secularists were not likely to give much attention to traditional Easter services. They learned that fact by "taking notes" on the surrounding culture. They concluded that people are becoming ritually self-sufficient: they want to be able to see, touch, feel, and "do" religion for themselves.

Since Easter was approaching, they decided to offer a 12-station journey that they called "The Veil." They invited about 30 people, representing all ages in the congregation, to create it. The experience included a rich variety of symbols, many adapted from the stations of the Cross. At one point people stepped through a torn veil, which went from ceiling to floor, representing the temple veil that was torn when Jesus died. The journey ended with a reflection area that surrounded a cross laid out on the floor. This nontraditional way of experiencing Good Friday and Easter drew many people, from church members to the unchurched. One of the attendees who came to faith in Jesus Christ said he never before had realized the depth of what Jesus did for him on the Cross.

RISK CONNECTIVITY

There's another piece to this present reality and, at first glance, it may seem to contradict the imperative of relevant worship services. But it's an absolutely crucial piece that we as leaders must not miss: worship is no longer the front door to the Church. It may be the second door people walk through, but it's certainly not the first—even in the spiritually curious context of the new millennium. Yes, there are those exceptional door-to-door mailers that might work for that small subset brave enough to negotiate the perceived hazards.

Is it possible, however, that mailers have been overused in the past two decades, that they can be an excuse for not being who we say we are: lovers of God and lovers of those God loves? Isn't it time that we risked getting to know ordinary people—no, extraordinary people—because God has put them in our path, not because they're in the crosshairs of an outreach program? Isn't it time that the first contact people make with us is our serving hands, not our logo and vision statement on trendy card stock?

We can't pretend that relational ministry (the only kind Jesus practiced) is easy. Certainly not at this particular point on the time line of human history. As each month passes in post-9-11 North America, we see a rising relational hunger, a desire to connect with others in significant and lasting ways. Unfortunately, that desire is dwarfed by a lack of both relationship skills and opportunities. Our gazebos, town squares, neighborhood drug stores, and mom-and-pop stores have vanished, and with them has vanished much of our relational repertoire. Parks have become havens for crime, while front porches—if even available—are usable luxuries only in gated neighborhoods.

If we imagine that communal amnesia is just an urban phenomenon, however, think again. As expanding seas of outward sameness, the nation's suburbs belie the reality of a disconnected diversity. According to the 2000 United States census, the following groups outnumber traditional families in our cities' peripheries: widows, single parents, non-Caucasians, 20-somethings living with parents, cohabiting adults (with and without children), and other such alternative family units. Cloned, particle-board havens—designed to perpetuate an isolated, self-sufficient lifestyle—are simply not built to handle the increasingly fractured, at-risk lives of the new census norm. In fact, they just might be a major contributing factor. Just ask the people in Littleton, Colorado. Columbine did not happen in a vacuum.

Bottom line: there's much talk about community in our increasingly community-starved world. But very few places and institutions in our society are actively promoting it. A few years ago, the authors of *The Cluetrain Manifesto: The End of Business as Usual* (Perseus Books) touted the Internet as the new watering hole: "We came to the web to find each other." That may be true. But what's also true is that we took the safest, most painless route possible. When daily we instant-message a cyber-acquaintance half way around the world but will go out of our way to avoid our next-door neighbor, we have a problem.

here's much talk about community... but very few places and institutions in our society are actively promoting it.

Real community comes at a price: the giving of ourselves to others, regardless of race, age, creed, or place in the demographic spectrum. Because of the One who has gone before us, giving His life as a ransom for all, real community is what the Church ought to do better than anyone else. Better than Starbucks, better than Budweiser, better than a U2 concert, better than chat rooms, better than eBay. The question is, are we ready to do "real church"? Are we up for a Rom. 12:1 kind of worship—one that's not frozen in the church mailer stage but offers our very selves as living sacrifices?

If we're ready to live the redeemed connectivity we claim, then here are a few principles for increasing connectivity in the area of worship:

1. *The creation of sacred space starts "out there"—beyond our four walls—not "in here."* If we can't create sacred space out there (that is, connecting with our neighbors, coworkers, and imperfect strangers in our everyday routines), then whatever we do on Sunday or on Wednesday night will ring hollow, even if we have all the bells and whistles—a 4,000-seat auditorium, a multi-million-dollar sound and video system, and a staff of 30. If you want to know how to begin creating sacred space beyond your church doors, see Steve and Janie Sjogren's *101 Ways to Help People in Need* and Brian McLaren's *More Ready than You Think*.

2. *Instead of inviting the unchurched into a "product," invite them into a process.* The intentionally unchurched are wary of

services that are mysteriously "created just for them" when no one has bothered to find out who they are. Note: we're not talking about demographic studies here. A better idea is to ask your friend—the same one you've been getting to know for a while now—to contribute ideas and artwork to your services. Common sense says that you probably won't have your friend lead worship. But you just might incorporate his or her black-and-white photos of street children.

3. Worship for community should be planned in community. How many of us as leaders practice the "cubicle approach" to planning worship services? We sit behind our desks with our own thoughts, biases, and defaults—pounding out the same kind of services year after year. We've dug deep ruts and cloned one kind of song medley for a month of Sundays. Isn't it time for a change? Isn't it time to invite more people, more learning styles, more variety of artistic expression into the process? If we're to have any chance of going Technicolor—the past fused to the present, the sounds of Edina, Minnesota, mingling with those of Edinburgh, Scotland—then we're going to need to gather a whole lot more colors for our paint box. Relax. You won't have to look far. There are people in your pews each week just sitting on their hands: artists, dramatists, sculptors, poets, graphic artists, animation experts. They're connected to a whole network of artists in your community, most of whom do not know Christ. You get the picture.

Get out of arms-length, program modes and risk relationship every chance you get. For worship that connects in every sense of the word, here are three radical steps you can take in the next quarter:

Before you design another mailer, challenge every person in your congregation including yourself to develop one significant relationship with a "non-church dweller" in the next three months. The minimum connection is doing something with that person twice monthly.

Before you even think about launching a special service geared to the unchurched, invite at least six people who fit that description into an ongoing conversation about what kind of faith experiences would be most meaningful to them. Meet in a local hang-out. Ask "what if" questions. Read their poetry and go to their art shows. Let them see your imperfections.

Finally, just say no to cubicle worship planning. Become a member of a multigifted, motley worship design community instead of an administrator of "the format." Give up control, and you'll give your congregation the gift of yourself.

What does "risking connectivity" look like in a church? One congregation in Colorado risked a time of reconciliation before everyone received Communion. The pastor read scripture about being reconciled one to another before we give our gifts to God (Matt. 5:23-24). He then said, "We're now on God's agenda; we don't care how long it takes." He made it clear that this was not an "Oh, by the way, go shake someone's hand" situation. Soon small groups of people began talking, praying, crying, and hugging. God's reconciliation impacted many lives. Two young men who had been estranged due to a longstanding disagreement, finally put down their guard and apologized to one another. The time of reconciliation took 12 minutes. For many people it led to the most meaningful time of Holy Communion they had ever experienced.

Another church has a formal liturgy. One Christmas Eve they risked connectivity by taking off their bracelets, watches, and rings, and putting them in a pile on the altar. They did this to symbolize that Christ came to us in pure humanity, with nothing but himself to offer, and so we likewise come to each other with no status. They held hands around the altar.

RISK PARTICULARITY

Looking out over the waves of same-shaped, same-colored houses in American suburbs, one is reminded of the way-too-perfect neighborhood in Madeleine L'Engle's *Wrinkle in Time* (Yearling Books). Children may not come out of the front doors at exactly the same moment and bounce balls in exactly the same rhythm as in L'Engle's vision. But the indistinguishable features in this country's new developments so vividly evoke L'Engle's scene that at times I've waited just a split second to see if the doors might really open.

Recently as I was driving north of Denver into one of its upscale bedroom communities, I saw an advertisement for a new kind of residential development. The billboard pictured five houses, all of unique designs and each painted in a different rainbow shade. The ad read, "Looking for an antidote to beige? Your search is over." Not to predict an onslaught of neon-colored houses, but this ad reflects a bold rejection of formula, predictability, and conformity. Evidently, many red-blooded Americans out there are getting tired of being a point on someone's graph, a number in someone's computer, a stereotype in some architect's prefabricated designs. The need for distinction and dissimilarity pervades many recent movies, including *A.I.* (Artificial Intelligence). Here, a robot "boy" spends the entire film trying to establish that he is not only unique among robots but loved precisely because he is unique.

What do Madeleine L'Engle, crayon-colored houses, and robots mean for worship? While many church leaders have been ridding our worship spaces of all visual distinction such as symbols, paintings, stained glass, sculpture, could it be that the people who are coming through our doors every week are sick to death of beige and are looking for an antidote? While we've been cloning our buildings, programs, language, and worship formats after a church located a thousand miles away, maybe the folks who sit in the seats in front of us want to know that they are unique and that their church is unique; that they aren't just getting warmed-over "McChurch"; that we as leaders love them as an unrepeatable representation of Christ's Body on earth, with unrepeatable gifts and flaws and an unrepeatable, peculiar destiny; that the reason we're their leaders is not because we were called to the ministry but that we were called to minister to and with *them*.

God did not create facsimiles. He did not establish His kingdom on earth by using industrial molds. God always creates and uses originals: matchless human beings and matchless communities, gathered to honor Him at a certain point on the time line and a certain point on the globe. When you meet in a local Thai restaurant with a 71-year-old poet, a 23-year-old mandolin player, and a 40-something interior designer and start crafting a Good Friday service, you risk particularity. When you ask a 19-year-old graphic artist—who happens to be a college dropout and is living with her parents—to create a digital backdrop for Pentecost, you risk particularity. When you use the angst-filled poem of a grieving 10-year-old (the one who lost his sister in a car accident two years ago) and you fuse it to a corporate reading of Ps. 63, you risk particularity.

There are no three-ring binders, no seminar notes, no workshop tapes that will tell the stories of the people God called you to serve, much less be able to connect those unrepeatable stories to God's story. This is your unsurpassed privilege: to risk particularity; to say a resounding "yes" to God's purposes and plans *in this place, in this time;* to work from the local outward, releasing yourself and your congregation from the bondage of sameness; to incarnate the gospel in all its marvelous specificity.

This is your unsurpassed
privilege ... to incarnate the gospel
in all of its marvelous specificity.

What happens when churches embody the value of particularity? They raise up their own artists, and the accompanying expressions in worship become their own. Photographers, painters, sculptors, and videographers become as important as singers and instrumentalists. The message is conveyed in every service that the days of formula and cloning are gone. We have opportunity to take from the best of what's out there, to gather around task and create sacred space, to work together to create something that's truly in our own verbal and aesthetic language. In the process, we get close to each other, and we can't resist sharing our stories with other.

I know of a church in uptown Chicago that's located inside a community of numerous artists and homeless people—some are in both categories. Artists and homeless persons have worked together to create murals on the side of their church building and to make stained glass windows together. The pastor told me that one homeless person will take another by the hand

and point to a mural or window, saying, "I go to this church; here's my piece."

A new church in a downtown Houston arts district did not hire a musician as their first staff person for worship, but a photographer. The church has built an area on premises where artists can have studio space. Everything there is created indigenously, from sculpture, woodwork, glasswork, painting, to much of the music as well.

A small congregation in a small Midwestern town decided to enlist the help of two teenage boys who had dropped out of the church a few years before but who had great video skills. Church leaders asked the boys to create a video about God's faithfulness in 95-year-old "Aunt Clara," who is now living in a nursing home. It was to be presented in church for an All Saints Day service. This was a church that had never done any form of video projection before; the boys had to travel 45 miles to rent a projector. They assembled a video collage of photos from the 100-year-old history of the church and interspersed them with various shots of Aunt Clara. After they put it together and showed it to the congregation, the unanimous response was "Why haven't we done this before?" So they did the same for Mother's Day.

This was a long-established church with a median age of about 65 years. If they can risk particularity, any church can because the concept spans many generations.

Risk reality, risk connectivity, risk peculiarity, because these are the God-carved dimensions of truly sacred space.

⚬7⚬

GREAT LEADERS TAKE RISKS
Knowing What Risks to Take When

Elmer Towns

All great spiritual leaders have taken risks of faith for the purpose of moving the work of God forward. I know of no great work of God that is not the result of someone taking risks, and I know of no effective Christian leader who has not taken the "If God doesn't help us, we're through" kind of risks. But the alternative may be worse—in the life of the church there's often more risk in doing nothing than in purposeful leading. However, God has given us leadership laws to take some of the "danger" out of risk. Or perhaps these principles are to reassure us that He will work through us as we take risks for the development of His Kingdom. Surely as spiritual leaders we often take what appears to be big risks from a human perspective. But the risks are not as threatening as they seem when we factor in God's principles, promises, and power.

BIBLE PATTERNS OF RISK-TAKING LEADERS

Scripture brims over with stories of risk-taking leaders. Look closely at the Bible, and you see how God stretched common people into effective leaders, starting with the establishment of the Jerusalem church. That congregation of new Christians started with 120 people meeting in an upper room in a private home. Soon 3,000 people were saved—that makes 3,120 people. Then Acts 4:4 reports 5,000 men were added—the Greek word translated "men" actually refers to heads of households—so it is possible the Early Church had as many as 25,000 to 30,000 in attendance in its beginning.

Later, Acts reports multitudes were saved, and before long

multitudes were multiplied. That's amazing growth. Serving that many people required leadership on someone's part. It also graphically demonstrates the need to dramatically increase the leadership pool as the church grows.

The Book of Acts, as we have seen, describes impressive church growth that always requires more and better leaders, though their requirements were somewhat different from ours since they had no church buildings. John Vaughan's research on megachurches found there were no sizable church buildings in the first 200 years of church history.

Interestingly, Vaughn cites an archaeologist's discovery of a large synagogue in Antioch that could hold 10,000 people. Apparently new congregations commonly used existing synagogues. Thus, churches at the beginning of the Christian era were often effective in leading people to Christ even though they had no buildings. They had God and each other but no buildings, no money, no canvassing, and no programs. God was enough.

MORE RECENT EXAMPLES OF RISK-TAKING LEADERS

Two millenniums of church history have taught us that Christians carried the gospel everywhere—literally to the ends of the earth. They wanted to conserve converts, to make the nurturing dimension (make disciples) of the Great Commission available to all believers. That meant starting congregations, so they planted churches. And new congregations meant that they had a continuous need for more and better leaders.

As the gospel advanced, the pattern of starting churches continued. In God's timing, the Good News reached the United States. Influential churches with large attendance were established in Boston, the country's first center of Christianity. Following the Revolutionary War, the center of positive response to the gospel moved to Philadelphia. From these and other centers the gospel spread like a well-fueled prairie fire into every territory and state of the union. Again, the success called for more and better leaders.

THE CHURCH'S LACK OF LEADERSHIP DEVELOPMENT

Though the church's development from Bible times until now called for new leaders in every generation, the purposeful teaching of leadership skills is a fairly recent idea in the church.

When I think back to the first churches I pastored, I realize I did not know much about leadership. I had no leadership training—none was available. Along with most of my contemporaries, I never heard one lecture and certainly never had an entire course on becoming an effective leader. Perhaps if our generation had the benefit of such leadership training, we could have done a better job in leading our congregations to dare to think big and to take greater risks for God.

These days, pastors must know more about how to lead than when I started due to the pressing needs and management of various ministries in the churches. And the good news is that many strong training opportunities are available. Most Bible colleges and seminaries offer leadership courses, and most require at least one course.

Effective leadership strategies are needed now more than ever before.

Leadership development opportunities are attainable to most pastors in a variety of venues near their homes. Books, tapes, and seminars are abundantly available. Magazines on church leadership are published by denominations and parachurch organizations. *Christianity Today* serves contemporary pastors so well with their magazine *Leadership*—I cannot imagine anyone trying to lead a church without reading every issue from cover to cover. John Maxwell and others offer contemporary pastors help for finding and applying leadership principles from Scripture. Cross-over leadership principles from business have also been helpfully applied to the church by many authors, publishers, and seminar leaders.

It's true—more information and more leadership training is more available now than ever before. It's also true that effective leadership strategies are needed now more than ever before. It's also true that church people expect more effective leadership these days because they have been exposed to good leaders on their jobs, in the community, and elsewhere. So more and better leaders are needed.

INCREASED NEED FOR AUTHENTIC LEADERS

Consider how the size and complexity of many contemporary churches have created the need for more effective leaders. Though some argue the smaller church is harder to lead that the megachurch, specialized leadership skills and the ability to develop strategies to meet those needs may not be too different in any size of church.

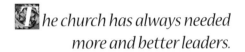

he church has always needed more and better leaders.

But here's the picture of today's megachurch movement. In 1968 only 98 churches in the United States averaged 1,000 or more in worship or Sunday School attendance. At that time I edited *Christian Life,* one of the largest-circulation Christian magazines of that period, where a listing of the largest-attendance churches in the United States was published annually. Out of that list, fewer than 100 had reached 1,000.

Today about 8,000 churches have more than 1,000 in attendance. Those churches are located in large cities as well as out-of-the-way places and everywhere in-between. Better leadership by pastors seems to be one of the key reasons for those impressive increases.

The multiplication of churches of various sizes plus adding new congregations keeps happening in every generation. As a result, the Church of Jesus Christ has congregations ranging from small house churches to much larger congregations like those mentioned in Bible times. That haunting refrain comes back again—the church has always needed more and better leaders. And it still does.

In the overall scheme of things, more leaders seem to emerge from congregations that were willing to take what seemed to be great risks for God. But more often than not, these risks turned out to be insignificant because those congregations sought and followed the guidance of God. Where He leads, He provides. And where a church follows His direction with wholehearted devotion, He empowers miraculous effectiveness.

EIGHT LAWS OF LEADERSHIP TO HELP REDUCE THE DANGERS OF RISK

In churches, like all other human organizations, everything rises or falls with leadership. Some risks, of course, come from aggressive leading. But let me share foundational leadership principles I mapped out in a kit called *Eight Laws of Leadership* designed to help minimize some dangers and risks.

1. The Law of Vision and Dreams

Without vision and dreams, a church or pastor is likely to have a sense of frustration about the present and fear of the future.

"By an act of faith he lived in the country promised him, lived as a stranger camping in tents. Isaac and Jacob did the same, living under the same promise. Abraham did it by keeping his eye on an unseen city with real, eternal foundations—the City designed and built by God" (Heb. 11:9-10, TM).

"Keeping his eye on an unseen city with real, eternal foundations"—how's that for being a visionary?

Listen carefully to these four words: no vision, no progress. Or to say it another way—no dreams, no new believer growth. Vision and dreams are significant—maybe "essential" is a better word—because they make a leader think through what the church can become and what God wants for its future.

George Bernard Shaw's well-known quote clarifies the importance of vision and dreams: "You see things, and you say, 'Why?' But I dream things that never were, and I say, 'Why not?'" (*Forbes Book of Business Quotations,* 281.) That's the reputation for dreams about one's church I wish every pastor had learned among his or her people.

In the vision phase of our work for God, in most situations the pastor is better able to dream and develop a vision than anyone else in the congregation. Why? The pastor is intensely involved in church life nearly 24 hours per day, probably has more training for ministry than anyone else, and knows the people. Thus he or she should be able to see farther than anyone else.

When people buy into a leader's dream, they buy into that person's leadership. It's a law of human behavior—people like to follow a leader who directs them to a goal they find desirable and believe achievable. Mark it down—you can count on it.

In so far as possible, visions and dreams should be based on solid, informed information. Business leader William Olsten explains, "Educated risks are the key to success" (*Quotable Executive,* 197.)

Consider the possible problems when an uninformed pastor proposes new ways for new days without reliable facts or expert opinions. In such a situation, decision makers may conclude their spiritual leader is an impractical dreamer with little common sense about money, people, and opportunity.

An example of informed visions and dreams is to understand and use the following six paradigms for churches regardless of their size (*Putting an End to Worship Wars; Into the Future*). As you read the list, you might ask yourself what kind of church you want your church to be. What is it now? And how could this information be used in my presentation for this month's board meeting?

- The *evangelistic* church. This church is intentional in outreach, designed to attract the unchurched, and focuses the entire congregation on winning the lost. Churches planted by Bill Hybels and Rick Warren are well-known examples.
- The *Bible expositional* church. This is a teaching church in which the main appeal of the public services is rational, didactic, propositional presentations of scripture. Churches led by John MacArthur and Charles Stanley are examples.
- The *renewal* church. This is a church focused on personal experience, where people expect to be stirred spiritually and emotionally.
- The *body life* church—a *koinonia* fellowship. Dr. Cho's congregation in Korea built on cell group is an example. This is the paradigm—called lay pastors—used by Dale

Galloway, founding pastor of New Hope Community Church in Portland, Oregon.

- The *liturgical* church. These churches focus on using creeds, written prayers, the arts, and classical-type music. These are likely to be Lutheran, Episcopal, or Presbyterian churches, among others.
- The *spiritual giftedness* church. This paradigm encourages people to take ministry roles based on their individual gift and abilities. The potential danger here is that lay Christians can miss the importance of pastoral leadership to provide overriding vision and spiritual motivation for the people of God.

reams provide hope and keep people believing in the church's tomorrows.

Remember this law of visions and dreams—and how to apply it. A church or pastor without a vision for the future often gets stuck giving energies to keeping the doors open and worshiping the past.

Dreams help keep your church focused on the future. They provide hope and keep people believing in the church's tomorrows. Often dreams help motivate a church to grow. And visions and dreams are always easier to communicate when they're based on information, trends, and facts rather than a mere whim, taste, or opinion.

2. The Law of Rewards

Without rewards, affirmation, and a sense of achievement, people tend to settle into mediocrity and lose interest in the future. Only the things that get rewarded get done.

The reward principle gives perspective to a leader so he or she sees beyond the barriers, the line of command, and/or the organizational flow charts to accomplishment, achievement, and satisfaction that comes from a job done well. The law of rewards brings the human element into the process.

Think how important appreciation, gratitude, and thanks

are to you. These are lovely affirmations that we all like to hear expressed about something we do or say. Sadly, some leaders find it easier to correct than to praise. Somewhere I read the delightful reminder that "gratitude" comes from the same root word as "grace," and "thanksgiving" has the same root word as "think." Showing grace and thinking thanksgiving makes any church a special place.

Leadership specialist John Maxwell explains the significance of a positive reward-affirmation process: "People do what you reward, not what you want, dream, demand, punish or even work for. You can count on people doing things that benefit them most. Do not reward the wrong activities. People work for money, time off, affirmation, leisure, glory, promotion, rest, and love."

Though it may surprise us, followers in any organization, and especially the church, behave according to what is rewarded. When positive attitudes, personal growth, spiritual reproduction, and imaginative creativity are affirmed and rewarded, these traits get multiplied in people's behavior.

But how are rewards to be provided in a volunteer-based organization like the church? Effective ways include praise/recognition; opportunities to learn and develop; expressed appreciation in public and in private conversations; encouraging people to do what they do best; and secondhand praise that means the leader tells someone else how much he or she appreciates the person's service—of course, the words always get back, just as you hoped they would.

Gratitude or appreciation is something every believer needs to receive from their spiritual leader. At the same time, every leader needs to be reminded that most people are wonderful, many are selfless, and in the church all are volunteers. Rabbi Joshua Heschel has a soul-stretching phrase that captures the benefit of affirmation and thanks for the leader, "gratefulness . . . for the gift of our unearned right to serve, to adore, and to fulfill. It is gratefulness that makes the soul great" (Dick Ryan, ed., *Straight from the Heart,* 75.)

Every church leader must face several realities that determine the effectiveness of his or her congregation. At any one time, some people are not doing things right. Some are not doing right things. Some are doing wrong things. Some are doing things wrong. And some are not doing anything at all.

The frequent response to all of this is to preach highly moralistic sermons and to accuse the whole congregation of apathy and lack of compassion. However, we know better, don't we? The most obvious way to get people moving from situations that are destructive to the Kingdom is to reward and affirm what they do well.

3. The Law of Credibility

Without credibility, the pastor-leader and believers make a mockery of the gospel. Evangelism, assimilation, fellowship— all significant components of church life—are worthless unless they are supported by integrity, confidence, and trustworthiness.

An authentic leader earns credibility because he or she knows the way *(knowledge)*, goes the way *(commitment)*, and shows the way *(example)*. A simple equation says it with simplicity: Knowledge + commitment + example = credibility.

Believable strategy is always a big part of credibility. People follow when they have confidence in the leader's life, character, and plan for the future. Leaders who believe in their followers have people who believe in them. In short, people will follow you when they believe you know how to get to the goal and that your walk matches your talk.

Beyond what the leader says is what he or she does. Noninterest, withdrawal from activities, and actual change of churches can often be traced to a noncredible act by either pastor or key lay leaders.

4. The Law of Communication

Faulty communication keeps a leader from sharing the meaning of the faith and from inspiring people with his or her dream for the church.

A few years ago I was with a young pastor who had listened to every John Maxwell tape and tried to do everything he suggested. The church was well organized, but it was not growing. I couldn't understand why until I heard him preach. He wasn't good up front. You have to connect with people when you get up in front of groups or in individual conversation. They want to know your heart and your vision.

Since communication by definition is the process of sharing information, thoughts, ideas, and opinions by speaking or writing, Christian leaders must be able to communicate effectively. Of course, that means the leader speaks accurately and interestingly, but it also means the communication process cannot be considered complete until someone has heard and understood. Thus, the Christian leader cannot allow himself or herself to think or say, *They know and understand because I said it.*

To be an effective leader, you must be able to communicate what you want followers to believe, where you want them to go, and what you want them to do.

Mere speaking never insures hearing, and even attentive listening does not guarantee understanding that results in favorable action. Former United States Vice President Hubert H. Humphrey once remarked, "The right to be heard does not automatically include the right to be taken seriously" (Louis E. Boone, *Quotable Business*, 59).

To be an effective leader, you must be able to communicate what you want followers to believe, where you want them to go, and what you want them to do. In any organization, most people are willing to follow a leader who knows where he or she is going, provided direction and inspiration are communicated effectively. One professor of preaching said, "Communication is God's delivery system for the gospel that works through the leader's conversations, sermons, writings, modern technology, and even body language."

Effective communication of meaning is a lifelong quest, even for the most gifted among us. The need for the Christian leader, then, is to be alert always to new ways of improving his or her communication and at the same time continually developing ways to be sure the other person really understands what the leader says and what he or she means.

5. The Law of Accountability

Human beings are prone to forget commitments and fail to follow through on assignments they have agreed to do at church.

Accountability is a multidimensional word that describes simultaneous responsibility in many relationships; so a man may be simultaneously accountable to his wife, children, parents, job, profession, and church. In a similar way, a pastor is accountable to church, family, profession, denomination, and community—to name only a few. And laity are fully responsible to their spiritual leader as well as to all the others on their list of responsibilities.

Our ultimate accountability, of course, is to God. Thus, an authentic leader helps an individual believer fulfill his or her growth potential as a Christian while reminding a congregation often that Christ is the Lord of the Church. That means Jesus is in final control and that all we do in and through the Church must be worthy of His full approval. And I rejoice in the awareness that some day I will answer to Him.

However, as shepherds of the flock of God with responsibility for the good of the church and for the development of individuals, it's necessary to hold ourselves and our laypersons accountable for their commitments of service. One of the best ways to get started with an accountability system at the church is for the leader to hold himself or herself accountable. Then congregants say that this pastor is serious about this matter, that they learned so much from watching their leader and that he imposes accountability on his or her own attitudes and actions. It is personally applying to our own ministry the advice of Paul to Timothy to "set an example for the believers in speech, in life, in love, in faith and in purity" (1 Tim. 4:12).

Accountability at church is not like punching a time clock at the factory or filling in a time sheet at the office. Rather, it's about giving of ourselves without reservation to God for His use and service. So the pastor-leader must remind the people of God whom he or she is working for. The time when the lay Christian in your church is most connected to Jesus is the time he or she will be most accountable to you. Try to remember always that laity have seldom been held accountable for assignments they have agreed to fill at church. So you may have to start slow with accountability. Stay firm. Laugh a lot, but don't give up.

After the smoke of confusion has cleared over your insistence on accountability, serious-minded believers want to have several accountability questions answered: *What am I to do? What am I to know? To whom am I accountable?* They want to know how they're doing. They want to know if they're living up to your expectations. And they want to know what they're achieving.

Accountability provides a tight connection of your church leaders with Jesus in the task of winning His world.

Accountability provides a tight connection of your church leaders with Jesus in the task of winning His world. Whether we realize it or not, accountability finally requires an evaluation of results. Too many in church spin their wheels for years in a mistaken muddle of misunderstanding that God honors faithfulness without concern for results.

While the measure of accountability in business is production and sales, the church's bottom line is character development and relationships that are being shaped into the image of Jesus Christ.

6. The Law of Motivation

Without lofty motivation, Christian service becomes perfunctory and is done for wrong reasons.

Serving the Lord is among the highest motivating forces in the world. Dee Hock, founder of VISA U.S.A., underscores what we already know but need to hear again and again: "Money motivates neither the best people or the best in people. It can move the body and influence the mind, but it cannot touch the heart or move the spirit; that is reserved for belief, principle and morality" (*The Quotable Executive*, 172). Think how far-reaching that concept is in challenging volunteers to serve God through His Church.

People are usually willing to follow a leader who gives them significant and inspiring reasons for doing the work. A giant step toward maximizing motivation happens when the leader understands and uses people's giftedness. Revisit the various church paradigms discussed earlier in this chapter under "The Law of Vision and Dreams." In each of these six paradigms, three factors are always at work: (1) gift colonization, (2) gift gravitation, and (3) gift assimilation.

Here's how these three gift dynamics work. When you consider these factors at a soul-winning church, it will be made up of a group of spiritually gifted people who love to bring others into relationship with Jesus Christ. Their dominant gift is evangelism, and these believers tend to attend churches where their gift is dominant and exercised.

Since teaching is the main focus over at the Bible church, those who have the gift of teaching are attracted to a colony of like-minded people. These churches often have people who left the congregations where they grew up and gravitated together to the teaching model. They say, "A thinking person's way of understanding God and the gospel is the way I want church to be."

In similar ways, some believers want to go where a church touches God in an emotional way. They become very expressive. Others like the small group. They wouldn't leave the small group for anything.

Thus, gift colonization simply means a leader understands how churches tend to emphasize one particular gift and how churches tend to focus mainly on one of the six paradigms listed earlier in this chapter. The term describes what is rather than what would be the ideal.

Gift gravitation means persons tend to gravitate to a church that exercises their dominant gift. And though they may not even be aware of their individual gifts, people tend to gravitate to churches where they feel useful and the emphasis is pleasing to them.

Now for the motivation and service components of this giftedness perspective. Gift assimilation signifies that a congregation finds ways to allow people to use their abilities in some strategy that's obvious to the newcomer.

Of course, there are hundreds of other motivation issues we don't have space to discuss, but for our purposes it's important that every leader keep asking himself or herself questions like

(1) What are my reasons for doing what I do? (2) What motive makes congregants act the way they do? (3) How can I challenge people to use their gifts in the most effective way?

7. The Law of Problem Solving

Problems, like weeds, get larger and more destructive with time. Thus, to ignore a problem because it seems hard to deal with today is to set yourself up for a bigger problem tomorrow.

United States President Lyndon Johnson sometimes used parables to make his point in conversations; reportedly he enjoyed telling a particular railroad story. As the story goes, a man applied for a job as flagman at a railroad crossing. Before he could be hired, he had to agree to pass a one-question test. The all-important job-defining question asked the applicant to imagine himself at a crossing that had one track with the Continental Express approaching from the east at 95 mph and the Century Limited speeding in at 100 mph from the west with only 300 yards between the two trains. Then the applicant was asked, "As flagman, what would you do?" He responded quickly, "I'd run and get my brother-in-law." Not understanding the answer, the examiner asked the applicant why. Replied the applicant, "He ain't never seen a train wreck." It's true—many pastors would rather watch a church wreck than do something to prevent it.

Like it or not, problem solving comes with the territory of being a pastor or spiritual leader. This reality is called "conflict management" in secular business literature. The idea is that in times of rapid change like ours, all organizations and especially churches are affected. As a leader, you need to help your congregation understand change, how it works, and how they can face it without unnecessary fear.

Three nonproductive questions are often asked or thought by leaders facing problems: (1) Why me? (2) Why now? (3) Why this? I suggest you save emotional energy and time by quickly moving past those questions because they keep you in a wheel-spinning mode of leadership.

I advise that you quickly move to three much more productive questions: (1) How big is the problem? (2) What do the people involved think the solution might be? and (3) What does the larger group—decision group or congregation—think the problem and solution are? In seeking answers to these questions, it's important to get as many facts as possible, to define and redefine your mission, and to give full consideration to all possible solutions.

As a leader, it's important that you communicate that you believe every problem has a solution. Unfortunately, many church lay leaders would rather discuss a problem than work for solutions. As a result, they retreat, surrender, withdraw, fuss, fight, or quit—all nonproductive attitudes.

Why not think of problem solving as an opportunity to strengthen the church and cement happy relationships between people? Done right, solved problems will increase morale, give people renewed confidence in leadership, and reinforce their understanding of the mission of the church.

8. The Law of Decision-Making

Without clear-cut, easy-to-understand decisions, an organization goes back rather quickly. Making no decision is sometimes as bad as making the wrong decision.

Nearly every Christian leader knows situations in which problems have multiplied across years until it was almost impossible to sort through the layers of issues, injured egos, and misunderstandings based on partial facts. Many of the most difficult problems faced by any congregation could have been easily solved at the beginning with a bit of effort and serious commitment.

The way to make good decisions is to follow this process, almost like a mathematical formula. Start with seeking God's solution through prayer and Scripture. Get a clear focus on all the issues. Define what needs to be done. Get as much information as possible. Consider every possible alternative, including some that may look impossible or even foolhardy. Discuss the issue with others. Seek input from those who will be impacted the most. Choose the best solution. Take time to make the best decision. Think through the consequences. Expect God to confirm your decision. And once the decision is made, make it work.

From beginning to the end of the decision-making process, keep your mind open to new possibilities. Sometimes the best solutions appear out of nowhere. And at times God works through the creativity of some person who is not in the inner circle of lay leaders.

Of the eight laws we've examined, vision, accountability, and decision-making are the most important. Build your skills on these laws. The most important thing a pastor does is not to preach but to make decisions.

Leaders make good decisions
on good information.

Leaders make good decisions on good information, bad decisions on bad information, and lucky decisions on no information. But when you have accurate information and wise perspective, decisions often seem almost automatic.

·8·

RISKS REQUIRED IN TURNAROUND CHURCHES
Disciple-Making Is the Key

Bill Easum

Most church leaders have had no training or experience in transitioning a church from dying to thriving. Don't let the unknowns deter you. People with a deep passion for mission can explore more of the edges of congregational life than they may think. Remember: innovation is not about skills—it's about passion for ministry.

Turning church members into disciple-makers—disciples who make other disciples—is one of the most pressing challenges of our time. Too many of our church members at best warm pews and at worst never attend worship or participate in mission. With the advent of a skeptical generation that demands authenticity, it's fair to say that Christians are the biggest obstacle to the expansion of Christianity.

WHAT NEEDS TURNING AROUND?

Church membership has nothing to do with being a disciple. A disciple is one who intentionally seeks to emulate Jesus in everyday life. This means someone who deliberately takes on the cause of Christ (Luke 9:23-25), puts Jesus before self, family, and friends (Luke 14:25-35); commits to world evangelism (Matt. 9:36-38); loves others (John 13:4-35); and abides in and is obedient to Christ (John 5:7-17). How, then, does a church leader go about developing disciples who make disciples?

1. **Most church leaders have to change their understand-**

ing of the role of clergy and paid staff. Eph. 4:12 reminds us that the role of church leaders is "to prepare God's people for works of service." This service is not "running the church" and going to meetings. The role of church leaders is more than just taking care of members. Their primary role is to provide an environment in which members can grow to be disciples who make disciples. They live and breathe, helping others grow in their faith rather than merely taking care of them. True, some people need to be taken care of. However, most people have within them so much more to give to the cause of Christ. Many are just waiting for the opportunity to stretch their spiritual wings. Church leaders who truly care about them give them that opportunity instead of keeping them dependent upon them.

The effective church leaders I have met in my travels are committed to four "BHAGs" (big, hairy, audacious goals). They risk just about anything to be part of carrying out the Great Commission. They focus their energy on developing the priesthood of all believers. They encourage people to seek God's gift within them through a process of discernment. They're rabid about the multiplication of everything important. In other words, growing people is more important to them than doing for people what they could be doing for others.

*By spending time with a few,
Jesus set the stage for others to
win many.*

2. Church leaders must realize that not all church members are or will become disciples, much less disciples who make disciples. This simple observation helps clear the way for church leaders to concentrate their time on the few who are ready for discipleship as well as to comb their acquaintances for people who are open to the possibility of becoming disciples of Jesus Christ. It's biblical for church leaders to concentrate most of their effort and time on a few.

Jesus spent most of His time with the Twelve. Often he zeroed in on Peter, James, and John. By spending time with a few, Jesus set the stage for others to win many. He knew He could do just so much. By multiplying himself, He could make a lasting difference. Like Jesus, pastors who want to make a lasting difference spend the bulk of their time working with people who are ready to take on responsibility instead of spreading themselves too thin. This group is always a small percentage of a congregation. This is in stark contrast to pastors in dying congregations who spend most of their time taking care of the equivalent of spiritual hangnails. Instead of starting spiritual fires, they spend time putting out fires.

3. **Pastors must become focused on the long-term vision of disciple-making instead of the day-to-day management of the church and the care of feeding the membership.** In doing so, the pastor does four things: He or she *(a)* consistently proclaims the good news in ways that are indigenous to the people in the area, *(b)* equips paid and unpaid staff to equip other laity "for works of service," *(c)* casts and guards the shared vision of the church, and *(d)* gets enough out of the way that others can blossom in their faith.

More important than what the pastor *does* is who the pastor *is*. The pastor is the spiritual leader of the church. The pastor's spiritual life and spiritual call are mutually reinforcing. He or she lives to be a role model for making disciples. This is far more difficult than just taking care of people.

4. **Staff members must be willing and know how to equip and empower people for ministry.** These people don't "do" ministry. They equip and empower others to "do" ministry and then coach them along their spiritual journey. Equipping and empowering are different. Church leaders often equip people but then fail to empower them. Empowering people means getting out of their way and allowing them to exercise the spiritual gifts within them without having to ask for permission. This way people grow in their faith instead of relying on the faith of those they hire.

5. **Empowered lay pastors are becoming the primary form of lay leadership.** In time lay pastors will be to the 21st century what the "minister" was to the 20th century. The criteria for lay pastors usually include the following: Lay pastors are called to a

ministry instead of nominated by a committee. They become lay pastors by feeling called to take responsibility for a ministry. They do not feel responsible to cast a representative vote on some future issue. They're also accountable to the pastor and the mission/vision/purpose of their particular church. They participate daily in prayer and Bible study. Monthly training and regular mentoring is a normal part of their service. (For information about lay pastors, see our web site—www.easumbandy.com—and search for Wesley Groups as well as Lay Pastors Manual.)

6. **Small groups that multiply and teams that produce are the places where most empowerment will take place.** The only people empowered by committees are those who already have power of leadership qualities. Spiritual wallflowers never blossom in committees. Multiplying small groups and effective teams brings out the latent qualities in people. A great website for small groups is www.smallgroups.com and, for team-based organizations, www.teamcenter.com.

7. **Discernment is more important than nominations and voting.** More and more churches are eliminating most if not all voting and relying on God to raise up the leaders and ministries needed. Spiritual gift inventories are replacing "dialing for people" encountered by most nomination committees when they call people to fill offices that nobody else wants to fill.

THE SCARY PART OF A DISCIPLE-MAKING FOCUS

Most church leaders have had no training or experience in making disciples. Management and decision-making have taken the place of disciple-making. When you look out over the congregation or go to a church meeting, how many spiritual giants do you see? Most pastors don't stay in one place long enough to know that most established church members have not grown spiritually since they were teenagers. This is not what God intended.

Making disciples can be a very threatening process for a pastor in an established church used to the pastor doing everything for them. Most pastors inherit a group of leaders who may or may not be disciples. Often one or two of them seem to be power hungry.

If you're in an unhealthy church, take a 20-year view of the situation. Realize that it will take several years to build a core of spiritual leaders. Cast your vision for a healthy church. Begin to work with the few who respond and nurture them in a small group as long as it takes. In the interim, work hard to get a few of the disciples in "official" places to make the process of decision-making easier. Move forward as the opportunity arises. The operative words are either "move" or "persevere."

If you feel in your gut there has to be more to vital ministry than you're experiencing at the moment, start the journey of faith and trust your instinct. Read on to discover ways to avoid some of the stress points that appear most often in transitional ministries and what leaders can do to reduce the stress.

How to Deal with Key Stress Points

Leaders and their spouses often face major stress when one or more of the following situations happen.

1. *When controllers are pressured to leave office.* We have seen very few turnarounds take place without a major changing of the guard. It's usually unwise to think that the same people who got the church into its current ingrown situation can lead it out of the mess. The number-one lesson I learned during several years of leading "Turn Around Seminars" is the importance of encouraging the pastor to gather and nurture a team of called, gifted, and equipped laity *before* beginning the turnaround. Only when the group appears biblically and spiritually mature enough should the pastor begin to prayerfully and lovingly replace the leaders. Often this process takes up to a year—and sometimes longer.

2. *When attempting either to change an existing worship service or begin an additional worship service.* I've learned from experience that the easiest way to turn around a church is to begin a new worship service designed in a way that today's person can hear the gospel. However, if the leaders have little clue about the essential mission of God's Church or if they prefer for the church to remain a cozy little club or family chapel, then conflict erupts. If the new service succeeds, the conflict often gets worse.

Turnaround pastors commonly hear these negative responses: "But we won't know everyone anymore" and "That kind of music doesn't belong in this church." These are unhealthy and unfortunate responses. How much better to grow healthy leaders who develop mission-shaped people who ask, "Does everyone in our area know God?" and "What kind of music will help people worship God?"

3. *When the pastor begins breaking the "personal chaplain" mold and begins trying to be a leader.* Such action always results in a shift in emphasis. Scripture's teaching is that the clergy equip God's people to do the ministry. For some reason the attitude in some churches is that "laity run the church and clergy do the ministry." We see very few churches turning around in which the paid staff does most or all the ministry.

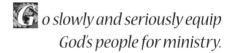

> o slowly and seriously equip
> God's people for ministry.

This transition also takes a lot of time. One of the best cures for opposition to lay ministry occurs when laypeople begin to experience the joy of doing ministry themselves as well as being ministered to by equipped laity. The key is to go slowly and to seriously equip God's people for ministry. Begin the process by training new people to expect laity to minister to them instead of the paid staff's tending to their every need. Next, begin to ask, "Who among our members will accept ministry from the hands of laity?" Let the laity minister to them while the pastor and/or staff continue to minister to those who expect you to play "pastor fetch."

4. *When the transition begins to cost money.* Most dying churches have money in the bank that they have saved for a rainy day. Such passion, though often misdirected, is understandable, especially for those who lived through the Great Depression. Churches with fewer than 125 in worship need to look for ways to implement the transition with as little cost as possible.

When I first came to the church I pastored for 24 years, we had very few people in attendance. I launched the turnaround without spending a dime, simply by spending as much time as possible out of the office and away from the flock but without losing the pulpit. It's possible for a pastor singlehandedly and within one year to bring 50 people into a small church, often even in sparsely populated areas. Such a number of additions can change the makeup of the entire church.

5. *When a desire for high commitment begins to encroach on the entitlements usually afforded to longtime members.* We know that the higher the standards placed on church leaders, the healthier the church becomes. However, making this shift causes conflict. Longtime members who feel entitled to all the benefits of membership become upset when encouraged to act like servants who exist on behalf of the non-Christian people around them.

This conflict often surfaces when leaders try to rearrange how the church spends money, targeting more of it toward non-Christians; or when paid staff begin devoting more time to non-Christians than to members; or when members are asked to park farther from the church to make room for visitors; or when some higher standards are applied to membership and leadership. Church leaders often find that they have to "grandfather" the longtime members and apply the new standards only to the new people coming into the church, at least at first.

6. *When new leaders make mistakes trying to implement the innovations.* The opposition uses the mistakes as an excuse to say "I told you so" and begins to stir up the conflict even further. The best way to deal with this stress: admit and celebrate the mistakes as a great time for learning instead of trying to justify the failed action.

7. *When churches with paid staff find that before the turnaround can happen, they must replace some long-term paid staff.* The staff who most often have to be replaced are the longtime secretaries who refuse to use 21st-century technology or who use their position to slow down the transition; the choir directors who try to sabotage the new worship services; or the part-time financial secretaries who tell less than the truth about the church's financial health, hoping that bad news will discourage people from starting new ministries.

ADVICE FOR TURNAROUND PASTORS

What else can you do to handle the added stress of a turnaround ministry?

Keep your own faith strong. Take time for regular Bible study and prayer each day. Get away from the church on a regular basis so you have space to dream and ponder and be filled with wonder once again. Keep in mind that congregations are seldom healthier than their spiritual leaders.

Embody servanthood. Establish this relationship before you start the turnaround so the majority will know your motives are not self-seeking. Everything about you must scream "servant."

Realize that turnarounds draw unbelievable resistance. Keep in mind that turning a church around usually involves spiritual warfare, not just differing opinions. Sometimes evil is the opposition. Most pastors don't understand this, or they underestimate it.

Be prepared for conflict. Never take opposition personally. You do not have this luxury. You must be the spiritual leader of the church even in the midst of conflict. If you respond personally, you raise the level of conflict beyond the ability to overcome. Instead, you must pray for the opposition. Learn from those who oppose you, but do not let them set the course for the church if you're convinced that the church must change or die.

Be realistic about your gift of mercy. Turnaround pastors are often called to choose between the mission of the church and the desires of individuals. People with high mercy gifts find this decision hard to make. They also tend to take things more personally than they can afford to do and survive the turnaround.

Give attention to growing people, not the church. Keep focused on developing spiritual giants instead of developing new programs or worship services. Developing spiritual giants takes lots of effort but in the long haul produces strong Christians who become key leaders in the church.

Settle job security issues in your mind before you start to make changes. Make sure you're secure enough not to worry about job security. If you're convinced a turnaround is what God wants, then if you lose your pulpit you can have confidence that God will open up another place for you to serve.

Commit to the long haul. Make sure you're in the turnaround for the long haul and that you're not going to jump ship at the first sign of mutiny. To do so destroys the hope of those who want change and increases the power of those who do not want change.

Prepare your new key leaders by not over promising and underpreparing them. Leaders need to know what to expect before committing to the turnaround. They should not be surprised by the responses.

Plan one or two quick victories. This is especially important in the smaller church. People need to have something to celebrate in the early part of the transition.

Revisit your call. After all of this, the best advice is to follow the passion of your call. If you sense transition is what needs to occur, start it. If you're not sure, or if you consider it only because so many of your colleagues are doing it, then forget it.

LEARN TO INNOVATE "ON THE FLY"

For the next 50 years, the ability to constantly innovate "on the fly" will present one of the most important leadership issues facing any organization. Not since the Reformation has the need to discover new ways to achieve old things been as important as it is today. Those not secure enough to innovate on the fly will be unable to effectively lead a church for very long. I make this claim for two reasons.

I see this ability in the pastor of every great church in which I have worked. Most pastors go through the motions, doing what pastors have done for decades, getting farther behind while often working harder. However, most pastors of growing churches with growing believers experiment with new ways to achieve old things. They seize on new opportunities instead of trying to solve old problems.

I also make this claim because of our world's present environment. The next 25 years or so will be remembered as a time of continuous ebb and flow, of disequilibrium. The phrase "radical change" does not adequately describe today's context. We live in a time of constant flux between extinction and birth. Some examples might help. Most jobs now driving the economy did not exist 15 years ago. Most jobs that will drive the economy 15 years from now do not exist today. Between 1980 and 1995, 44 million jobs disappeared, while 77 million new jobs were created. During the same period, every mainline denomination declined in strength while new associations of congregations emerged, such as the Willow Creek Association, the Vineyard movement, Hope Chapels,

Calvary Chapels, Leadership Network, the growing alliance among postmodern pastors, and many emerging urban-oriented parachurch groups. Many staff positions that churches will need 10 years from now do not exist today.

> *eaders of effective churches don't just tolerate change— they build it into the fabric of their ministry.*

Deconstruction has replaced evolution. The epistemological and ontological foundations of the world as we know them today are breaking down and giving way to new ways of perceiving reality and processing knowledge. Everything on which the industrialized, modern world was based is being destroyed. We live in a world between rules. By the midpoint of the 21st century, a new foundation for civilization and community will be constructed and new rules recognized. In such a world the most fatal remark one can make is "We've always done it that way." About the time we get something down pat, the world no longer needs it. The laptop computer on which I write these articles could symbolize this ebb and flow. Although it's less than six months old, I've already started looking for its replacement.

Innovating on the fly means living at the edge of chaos without becoming part of the chaos. Leaders who seek harmony and equilibrium will lead churches that stagnate and die. Like an organism adapting to the ecosystem's constant changes, leaders of effective churches constantly test the edges of church life. They don't just tolerate change—they build it into the fabric of their ministry.

Effective leaders today reside somewhere between absolute order and absolute chaos. The trick is to ride the wave of chaos to its crest without becoming engulfed by it. Instead of seeking order, leaders count the chaos. The worst thing leaders can do today is to avoid the chaos of the moment for the order of the past. To do so signs one's death warrant as a leader and consigns the organization to death.

I have learned some clues along the way to share with those who want to be part of God's working at this time in history.

Innovation Clue 1: Keep anchored in Jesus. For constant innovation on the fly, the leader must be firmly anchored in Jesus. I have seen only one anchor that sustains Christian innovators in times of real turmoil: a deep, personal, life-changing, ever-renewing commitment to Jesus Christ. No prestigious office, salary, or fame can provide the kind of sustenance and stamina that the next 50 years of Christian history will require. If we lose our Christ-connected core, we have nothing worthwhile to share. Make sure your relationship to Christ is firmly in place.

Innovating on the fly does not signify a skill one possesses. Rather, it's a passion arising from one's commitment to a mission. Christian innovators so desperately want to communicate God's message that they don't fear trying new things and making mistakes as long as they learn new ways to accomplish old things. The stronger our anchor is in Jesus Christ and the mission He left with us in His last will and testament (Matt. 28:19-20) and His post-last will and testament (Acts 1:8), the more easily we can innovate and live with the ensuring chaos. When they can no longer achieve the mission, innovating leaders desperately look for new ways to achieve it. Don't be afraid to make mistakes and learn from them.

Our society will find anchors in short supply over the next 50 years. The fragmentation, disequilibrium, and uncertainty of our time will make for a rough ride. The goal of innovation for a church leader is not to create something new but to find new ways to achieve something old—Christian reality and community.

Innovation Clue 2: Go for the big, hairy, audacious innovations. Be bold. Small innovations equate to little more than tinkering. Fiddling with small changes just keeps everyone in an uproar. Study the big picture of your church's potential and mission. Share a realistic vision of what your church can become, and watch thinking people respond.

Innovation Clue 3: Never stifle an innovating moment— even if you're not sure if it is the thing to do. I remember returning from vacation to find a note on my office door from one of the preaching pastors: "Bill, wear blue jeans Sunday morning to worship. We're going to wear them all summer." At the time I thought this "dumb idea" would cause lots of trouble. Today it's normal dress in many postmodern churches.

Innovation Clue 4: As soon as you perfect what you're doing, move on to something else. Don't hang on too long to something working very well. Keep looking for ways to improve what you do, or move to the next level. The old adage "Don't let go of what you have until you have something new to grab hold of" simply does not mean much in a turbulent environment. You must have great discipline and are constantly seeking to place yourself where God works in the world. The trick at the top: keep perspective and see over the horizon. Being at ease in Zion remains the worst enemy of innovation.

Innovation Clue 5: Gravitate toward the edges of your religious group, because innovation has less resistance there. You'll never find the status quo at the edge, nor will you hear "We've never done it that way before." Maximize your edges by reading in areas outside of your discipline, attending events not sponsored by your denomination, networking with pastors in other traditions, talking with your kids, or visiting a new web site.

Innovation Clue 6: Listen to your instinct, not your critics. During the first 20 years of my ministry, I received a lot of criticism from all fronts. They said I was doing everything all wrong, even though my churches grew. At one point a bishop collected signatures to get my ordination revoked. At another time this same bishop tried to get a major seminary to drop its teaching relationship with me. All because I innovated on the fly. Now I find it hard to stay home enough because so many denominational officials consider what I advocate to be the wave of the future.

All along I felt in my heart that I was going the right direction, but surely so many of my peers couldn't be wrong. For a short time I listened to them too much, which caused me to waste some of my earliest years. However, it soon became clear that what I was doing caused my church to grow and what they advocated caused their churches to decline. So I began to follow my heart and simply tune them out.

As a result, the church I served for 24 years was one of the first congregations in the United States to do a number of things: It required months of training before allowing teachers to enter the classroom, offered two or more preachers every week from which to choose, put computers in the Sunday School, offered multiple worship services, considered small groups as the hub of the church, had a social-justice ministry that attacked the root causes of social injustice in our city and state, and had one of the first strongest permission-giving lay ministries in the 20th century.

A WORD OF WARNING AND ENCOURAGEMENT

One thing about innovative leaders: they tend to gather around themselves other leaders who may or may not be innovative but who thrive in continual movement into the future instead of a static reproduction of the past. When a person who is not a leader replaces an innovative leader, three things always seem to happen: the innovation stops and maintenance begins, the leaders in place when the innovator left begin to leave because they no longer feel challenged, and non-innovative, past-oriented people move into the vacuum and take the organization back to a state of equilibrium. Innovative leaders must replace innovative leaders.

I began this chapter by stating, "Turning church members into disciple makers—disciples who make other disciples—is one of the most pressing challenges of our time." I also claimed that "Christians are the biggest obstacle to the expansion of Christianity."

The good news is that they—and we—don't have to be. What kind of disciples will step out of your church? The answer may rest in what you do next.

This chapter was adapted from Bill Easum's articles in Net Results, *a monthly journal of "New Ideas in Church Vitality." Bill Easum is president of Easum, Bandy & Associates. He can be contacted by E-mail at easum@easumbandy.com.*

▪ 9 ▪

HOW TO RAISE MONEY AND FAITH WITHOUT SINKING THE SHIP
Making God Your Source
Dale Galloway

This chapter is designed to build your faith. It's about trusting God for bigger financial gifts for the enlargement of the work of God—and making sure your local congregation doesn't sink financially in the process.

My friend Gene Appel, senior minister of Central Christian Church in Las Vegas, Nevada, recalls the first time he ever asked anyone for a major financial gift to the church. He asked a certain couple to meet with him, and they instead invited him over for dinner. During the meal he cast the vision for the relocation project that the church would soon be entering.

"How are you going to finance it?" the husband asked Gene.

"Funny you should ask," Gene replied. He spoke of involving as many people in the congregation as possible. Then he added, "We really need people to do some upfront leadership gifts to set the pace for the congregation. That's why I'm here—to ask if you would prayerfully consider giving a gift between $50,000 and $1,000,000."

Without missing a beat, the husband replied, "Well, you can count us in for a million."

Gene just about fell onto the floor. This was the first time in his life he had ever asked for a gift like this.

An hour or so later, it was time for Gene to head home. Still lightheaded from the astounding promise of the huge donation,

107

he thanked them again as he put on his coat. He thanked them once more as they walked together onto the front porch and yet again as he went down the walkway. Finally, for his last word as he climbed into his pickup, he said, "Thanks a million!"

Both he and the host family burst out in laughter at his unintended humor, and then he drove away.

Trusting God When Doing "The Ask"

Not everyone receives a "yes" the first time, as Gene Appel did, especially when sizable donations are at stake. But most church leaders do get involved personally with lead donors. "I never saw myself as a fundraiser beyond preaching each year on stewardship," Gene says. "But I knew for our relocation project, I was going to have to personally tap some people on the shoulder who appeared to have some financial means."

If God is my starting point, then anything is possible.

As with most church leaders, I, too, discovered early that I need to do "the ask" in person and face-to-face. I first realized this principle in 1972 when preparing to launch my lifetime dream—"a church for the unchurched thousands" that became New Hope Community Church of Portland, Oregon. I prayerfully made a list of people who might provide some financial start-up support. My other chapter in this book explains that when I had finished sharing with all of them, I still had no money. I felt discouraged and beaten. I even made the added mistake of blaming some of these good people for their failure to respond the way I thought they should.

Then I realized the most important lesson about "the ask"—that I was wrongly looking to people to be my source of financial supply. What a transforming day it was when I discovered that I needed to make *God* my source. If God is my starting point, then anything is possible. God works through people. While it certainly helps to ask them face-to-face, my trust must remain totally in God as my provider.

Otherwise I worry. Every time I forget who my Source is, I begin to fret. As Oswald Chambers said, "All our fret and worry is caused by calculating without God."

Big Dreams Attract Big People

A second principle to remember is that money follows vision. Money flows to vision. Big dreams attract big people. God's people give to causes that use their money effectively for things they love. Build people, make disciples, and you will raise up givers. As Jesus promises, "Give, and it will be given to you. A good measure, pressed down, shaken together and running over, will be poured into your lap. For with the measure you use, it will be measured to you" (Luke 6:38).

Ray Cotton, now pastor at New Hope in Portland, learned this principle early in his ministry when he was pastoring Central Community Church, Wichita, Kansas. As he says, "Tithers love to tithe, and big-gift donors love the blessing they receive from making a faith-stretching gift far beyond their tithe."

During a major building program in Kansas, he brought in a financial consultant who talked about the importance of finding a major lead-gift donor. "There's got to be someone in the congregation who could give a million dollars," the man told Ray. "No, we don't have anyone with that ability," Ray replied. "All I can suggest is that we visit one person who might have the potential to give half that amount."

Ray made the appointment saying, "The reason I'm coming is to talk about the finances for the new facility." The man was very gracious in receiving his pastor. Ray looked at him and said, "We've got to make the project believable. People are excited but don't have the faith that it will really happen. We need a lead gift of $500,000." Ray stuttered on that last sentence. He felt so intimidated to ask this man who appeared so successful and wealthy.

The man looked at Ray and then laughed. Ray didn't know why, so he stayed silent.

"Pastor," he said, "I really believe in the vision and what we're doing, but I can't give you a half million dollars. I don't have anything near that amount. In fact, in the next 90 days we're facing a critical juncture in our company. I'll either go bankrupt or we'll turn a corner."

Ray was feeling so disappointed that he almost didn't hear the next thing the man said. "Actually, Pastor, I'm put out that you asked so little. If we do well, I'll give you a million dollars."

Ray didn't know anything to do besides pray. Together they asked God to bless this man's company so that he could provide a huge gift toward the church's expanded facilities.

They hugged and said goodbye.

Three months later, Ray went back to his office and picked up a check for $1.2 million. In his wildest imaginations, Ray could not have dreamed that this would happen. He truly could join with the apostle Paul and say, "Now to him who is able to do immeasurably more than all we ask or imagine, according to his power that is at work within us, to him be glory in the church and in Christ Jesus throughout all generations, for ever and ever! Amen" (Eph. 3:20-21).

Years later, Ray reminded me that it wasn't just him and the church who received the blessing. "The guy I leave back in the office is a lot more happy and blessed than the recipients are. That's why Jesus said it's 'more blessed to give than to receive,'" he explained, referring to Acts 20:35.

Giving Is Contagious

When the church you serve begins to receive large donations, they will probably not be one-time gifts. Not only do previous donors want to trust God with additional gifts, but sometimes the experience is contagious across the congregation.

One of my joys as dean of the Beeson Center at Asbury Theological Seminary is to mentor annual groups of Beeson Pastor doctoral students and then to hear stories of what God has done after they return to full-time ministry. One of my former students is John Edgar Caterson who became senior associate pastor at Princeton (New Jersey) Alliance Church where Bob Cushman is senior pastor.

In early 2000, Bob launched a sermon series in which he challenged the congregation to seek God multiple times saying, "Speak, Lord, I am listening and I will obey," taken from Eli's words to young Samuel.

The sermon said nothing about money or finances. Yet that is how God used the message with a couple who had never given their church a large or unexpected financial gift, although they had known about some of their friends at church making large gifts.

The week after the sermon, the husband sent Bob this E-mail: "On Sunday you challenged us as a congregation to spend the next 20 days asking God what He would have us to do. I didn't need 20 days to know the answer to this question, since I have felt for a long time that God had a task for my wife and me. In fact, it was heavy on my mind before I came to the worship service that morning without knowing the content of your message."

The E-mail concluded by saying that "in a few days" the church would receive a check in the mail for $1 million to help pay off the newly finished facility. It arrived as promised, with "Yeah, God!" shouts echoing down the halls by everyone who heard about it.

Setting a Personal Example

April 24, 1974, is a day I'll always remember. I had the breathtaking excitement to be holding my wife Margi's hand as our oldest child, Ann, was born.

Even the hospital bill couldn't dampen our joy as we prepared to take her home. Our health insurance covered everything except $500, but due to some other unexpected emergencies, we had only $55 available for payment. The hospital agreed that I could have 90 days to pay the remaining $445.

All too swiftly the days came and went, and suddenly it was day 89. With the extra expenses of a new baby, we had not been able to squeeze out $10 extra, let alone $445.

On that Thursday morning during our family prayers, Margi reminded the Lord that we had endeavored to put Him first in everything. We had applied Matthew 6:33—"But seek first his kingdom and his righteousness, and all these things will be given to you as well." As I left for the office, Margi reiterated her unquestioning belief that God was going to take care of us. Throughout the day, I thought about our pressing need, prayed about it, and then thought some more.

That evening, I received an unexpected phone call from a realtor. He represented a client who wanted to buy a sewer easement along our home property in order to develop some land behind our house. We set an appointment for the next morning.

The young man arrived promptly at my office, introduced himself, sat down, and told me his client would give me $250 if I would simply sign over the easement. "Lord, what should I do?" I prayed. "This is only half the money we need."

I took a deep breath and said, "I would be happy to sign for $500." He checked with his client and in 20 minutes reported, "My client will pay you the $500 immediately if you will sign now." We paid the hospital $445, gave our $50 tithe to God, and had $5 left over for a family treat. Together we thanked the Lord for supplying our every need.

Job Hunting on the South Side of Chicago

Does similar faith show up in communities that are hard hit economically? What about people who are struggling just to keep their doors open? What about countries where Christians are persecuted?

A few years ago, I visited Salem Baptist Church on Chicago's South Side. It is a difficult area. I saw people's needs met as the Body of Christ responded in faith.

During the prayer meeting, they not only prayed for their people who needed jobs, but they matched them up with people who had job leads. They even paid to get a member family's house out of foreclosure and then took them through a debt-counseling program. What they don't have resources for as individuals, they see God provide through the church as a whole.

God is too good to do bad,
too wise to make a mistake,
too strong to fail, and too
interested to ignore us.

Whether it's $500 for your family or $500,000 for your church, no money problem is so great that it can't be overcome. Like a father who gives good gifts to his children, God delights in giving the very best to His children. As Jesus said, "If you, then, though you are evil, know how to give good gifts to your children, how much more will your Father in heaven give good gifts to those who ask him!" (Matt 7:11).

Make God your source, and anything is possible. God is too good to do bad, too wise to make a mistake, too strong to fail, and too interested to ignore us. To be God's child is not to be without problems but to face problems, to learn from mistakes, to turn mountainous problems into mountainous successes of faith.

Set a personal example by how you trust God to provide. You don't have to cook yourself in a stew over money problems. Wherever you have a need, that's where you can look for God and find Him every time. He wants to supply your need.

Simple principles, based on the Word of God and applied to your ministry, can reap marvelous results.

Should We Borrow or Not?

What about borrowing money? Does a risk-taking faith invite a congregation to go into debt, or should it trust God to provide the funds in advance?

If you sense a strong need to borrow, be sure to draw upon wise financial advisers in your community or congregation. They can help you calculate an appropriate maximum debt load, if any, for the congregation.

My experience is not to let your debt load exceed more than one-third of your income. Otherwise, the risk is too precarious. You don't want to overstress your people. You don't want to have to cut staff or your operational budget to make the monthly payments, which would keep you from servicing people or reaching out to the lost. You always want to avoid a survival mentality.

My overall advice on borrowing comes from Robert Schuller's book *Your Church Has Real Possibilities* (27). He says, "Don't be afraid of debt, but understand what debt is." Then he illustrates it with a personal story. As a young pastor in Chicago, he lived in the church parsonage that was heated with coal. In October he needed coal for the furnace. One of the longtime members of the church told him he would need about five tons of coal to get through the winter. At $15 a ton, the bill would be $75.

Schuller didn't have $75, so he called the coal yard to ask if he could charge it. They said no.

He went to a bank and asked for a $75 loan to buy coal.

They turned him down. After Schuller pleaded for an exception, the banker said, "All right—I'll loan you money for coal this time, but never again."

"Why not?" Schuller asked.

"You'll burn up that coal," the banker explained. "If you don't pay us back our $75, what do we get in return? Nothing—it's all gone up in smoke."

That banker gave Schuller an insight he's kept for years: If you have to borrow, do so for things that have collateral, nondepreciable value. Borrow for a new building to house the growing youth group but not for the fuel to heat the building. Borrow for a new van to transport the seniors group but not for the gasoline to put into that van. "We don't borrow money for our television ministry, for interest on the capital debt, for salaries or for utilities," concluded Schuller. "That's like borrowing money for coal" (28).

WHEN YOU'RE CONSIDERING WHETHER OR NOT TO BUILD

When you're thinking about construction, be sure to build on your strengths as a congregation, not your weaknesses. For example, before you expand your facility, go to multiple services so you have more people and more resources for the bricks-and-mortar parts of construction.

When you're planning to build, you don't want to overbuild. Empty seats will kill momentum. I have seen too many churches who have overbuilt only to see their sanctuaries half full.

Also, don't cut back from doing multiple services, because you will lose 15 to 20 percent of the people immediately if you do.

Risking in faith is not like jumping off a building. There's a law of gravity that guarantees that you'll be hurt if you jump off the top of a building. Instead, risking in faith involves building on one step at a time. You break down the huge project into doable steps. You take one step and achieve that, and then you step out in faith again. You keep building on what you have already achieved to carry you into the next step of the future.

In that way you'll raise money and faith but not sink the ship.

10

HEALTHY RELATIONSHIPS: THE FOUNDATION FOR RISK-TAKING

The Art and Heart of 21st-Century Leadership

Wayne Cordeiro

Read Eph. 4:11-16 and circle all the words that require a foundation of healthy relationships in your congregation:

[God] gave some as apostles, and some as prophets, and some as evangelists, and some as pastors and teachers, for the equipping of the saints for the work of service, to the building up of the body of Christ; until we all attain to the unity of the faith, and of the knowledge of the Son of God, to a mature man, to the measure of the stature which belongs to the fullness of Christ.

As a result, we are no longer to be children, tossed here and there by waves and carried about by every wind of doctrine, by the trickery of men, by craftiness in deceitful scheming; but speaking the truth in love, we are to grow up in all aspects into Him who is the head, even Christ, from whom the whole body, being fitted and held together by what every joint supplies, according to the proper working of each individual part, causes the growth of the body for the building up of itself in love (NASB).

I find an important leadership nonnegotiable principle in this passage. It speaks to the heart and art of 21st-century leadership. If glossed over or de-prioritized, this issue will cause untold grief in years to come and relegate your ministry to its most elementary stages. It tells us that we cannot go forward—that God cannot do miracles of life change in our congregation—until we lead the way to restore broken relationships and snagged friendships.

Getting to the Heart of the Need

I was in a restaurant some months ago having breakfast when a pastor came up and asked, "Wayne, can I sit with you?"

"Absolutely," I said, so he sat down. He looked at me over the table and said, "Give me a new program to spur on my church. Our church is lethargic, and we just need to get them off dead center. Please give me a new program, a new idea, a new video—something."

I said, "Let me start with a basic question: How's your church?"

"It's coming through as well as can be expected," he replied. He commented that he was new as the pastor.

Then he explained how the former pastor had resigned. "One Sunday morning the pastor came up to the platform, looked over the congregation, and said, 'Could I have the elders and the board members stand?' They stood up. Then he said to the congregation, 'It's because of these people that I'm resigning the church.' Then he took his Bible and left."

It took me a minute to get over the shock of that account. I needed to hear more details of his situation, so I commented, "You know, things didn't fall apart just on that Sunday. I suspect it happened a year or two before when healthy relationships in the church were given less importance, and broken friendships became acceptable. It merely came to a head on that Sunday."

After hearing more of this church's story, I was ready to respond to the pastor's original question. "Here's your assignment over the next six months," I said. "Don't initiate any new programs or new techniques. Instead, go on a crusade against broken relationships and snagged friendships. Look every person in the eye, and if you detect even a hint of hurt, a hint of unresolved relational issues, anything that has somehow gone underground, do not pass go, do not collect $200—stop and repair it. Start with yourself. Ask all your leaders to do the same thing with you. That's your 'program' for the next six months."

"If there are broken relationships," I said to him, "and they're being tolerated and people have harbored enmities between one another, the body can't build itself up in love. I will give you a secret, Pastor. You can go to 100 seminars and get all the best programs and the best techniques, but if there are broken relationships and unhealthy relationships in that local body, then no program will fly, not even the best one. The people will make sure it doesn't fly. They'll sabotage that program."

Go on a crusade against broken relationships and snagged friendships.

My breakfast guest nodded, showing that he caught the idea.

So I continued. "On the other hand, if there are healthy relationships in the church and people are excited to be with one another, and there are no enmities and no unresolved issues, then any program will fly. Even if you had no programs, if people were just excited about being with one another, do you know what will happen? Because of the condition of the soil, fruit will start to burst forth. The gifts in the Body of Christ will just start popping up, and it will self-organize if there are healthy relationships. But if not, you will work like a dog to organize, and it won't fly."

This pastor and I agreed that ministry follows the principles of planting and harvesting. It's like a farmer conditioning the soil before planting new seeds. If the farmer has secured the best seed from the market but has hardened soil, weedy soil, shallow soil, rocky soil, or even untreated and unconditioned soil, it won't grow anything. Even if a seed does survive the bad condition of the soil when it grows, it'll grow up mutated and stunted at best.

It's the condition of the soil, the health of the environment, that affects the fruit. When you have healthy relationships and you work from there, that's like conditioning the soil.

Life Instead of Death

A year ago, I took my family to the Opryland Hotel in Nashville. It's a fascinating place with 15 acres under roof. It was the middle of summer and extremely hot outside. The inside, though, was temperature controlled and humidity-regulated, with tropical plants like those we have in Hawaii. I was amazed. When you went outside those glass doors, it was like checking your turkey at Thanksgiving in the oven.

Inside what would have died under glass and extreme heat was thriving. What should not grow was healthy and vibrant and fruitful. I looked at that and thought, *What a picture of the church!* No new programs will fly without the conditions of growth. No new incentives will be fruitful without the condition of fruitfulness.

Here's the secret that will save you thousands of dollars trying to get new programs. If relationships are poor and snagged friendships go tolerated and unresolved, then you can bring as many programs back as you want, and they won't fly. On the other hand, if there are healthy relationships, even the most remedial programs will be defined. The homeliest programs will become glorious. There will be alchemy of divine intent that will change even the simplest efforts into something so profound and life changing. It's the condition of the soil.

The same is true with my body. If I'm healthy and I don't carry around the toxins, stress, and adrenaline overdose, then I rarely get sick. When I do get sick, I heal very quickly and bounce back tomorrow. But if I have stress, anxieties, and fears, I make my body very susceptible to illness. My adrenaline turns into toxins. Tumors, cysts, and acid may develop. The body does not heal in the presence of stress.

Before you examine any program for your congregation, the best thing you can do is to stop and make sure that your congregation is healthy, with no broken relationships, no unresolved issues, no snagged friendships.

Relational Health Begins with You

Once a young man came up to his wise pastor and said, "Preacher, we need revival in this place. God hasn't been moving in this church." As the young man continued talking, the old pastor took a piece of chalk and started drawing a circle around the young man as he griped and complained.

The young man stopped and asked, "What are you doing?"

The pastor replied, "When revival starts in this circle, revival will start in this church."

Relational health begins with the one reading this book. We need to be the ones to initiate the repair. When I consult with a church, I seldom look first at its organizational charts and programs. You know what I look at first now? I look at a church's capacity for healthy relationships. It's not that the other aspects of organization are unimportant, but they are not primary.

The power of a church will be found in the capacity generated by healthy relationships. Spiritual power comes not from organizational charts or tasks or hierarchies or manuals but from the things fundamental to building healthy relationships. Do people know how to listen and speak to one another? Is there an obvious basis of trust among the leaders and people in the church? Can people work well in teams? Are the times of celebrating with one another often or infrequent? Is there a respect for people regardless of their position or role? Is a spirit of teachability exhibited? When correction needs to be given or received, is there receptivity? Do people of greater authority and skill work well with those who may have less authority and skill? Does each individual leader have a daily devotional time with the Lord Jesus Christ so that he or she is personally growing in Him?

Spiritual power comes ... from the things fundamental to building healthy relationships.

The larger a church grows, the more emphasis and time must be invested in maintaining healthy relationships and keeping the soil conditioned. As a congregation and staff grow in size as well as in age, they'll find more baggage, more history, more opportunities for stepped-on toes. If you're not careful, you'll walk right on without repairing anything. You will leave limping relationships in your path. The stronger the relationships, the greater the capacity and potential for ministry. If you have a breakdown of relationships between people, watch for fallout with your programs.

How God Broke Me

Mark was one of my greatest board members. In fact, when we built our first building in the first church that I pioneered, he was the one who led the charge. He was my stalwart right arm.

After 10 years, all of a sudden Mark started to turn against me in board meetings. Anything that I wanted to implement he wanted to get rid of. If I said it was green, he said it was orange. Everything I did he would sabotage and then would get other people to sabotage as well.

I asked myself, *What is wrong with this guy?* I couldn't figure it out. Soon enough I became more than a little miffed at this guy. It was eating me alive.

I'll always recall the breakthrough. I was praying one Saturday morning, and the Lord said, *You go make it right.*

I replied, *Lord, me make it right? It's his fault—he's the idiot. I'm the one who's right.*

The Lord replied, *It doesn't matter. You go make it right.*

I got into my car and drove to his house, praying, *God, please don't let him be at home. I want to obey You, but I don't want to go through this.*

I knocked on his door. As he opened the door, his eyes got big, and so did mine. I thought, *What do I do now?*

" Mark, may I come in?"

"Yeah, come on in."

So I went in, and we sat down. As we talked, what came out was something I was blind about. He said, "Wayne, when we first started this church, you would call me once in a while. You'd at least have lunch with me. But the church is too big now. I feel like you don't even know my name. You have no idea what I'm going through. My wife was in the hospital. You didn't even know. My kid got into an accident. You didn't know."

As he began to enumerate some of the sufferings that he was going through that I was oblivious to, I was breaking inside.

After listening for a long time, I said, "Mark, would you stand up?" He stood up, and I said, "Will you please forgive me?" He began to cry, and so did I. We hugged and wept on each other's shoulder.

A miracle happened that day. God spoke to my heart about

allowing relationships to go bad. When you see the warning signs, stop and repair them, because the capacity of healthy relationships will be the power of a church. You may need to write a note. You may need to make a phone call. You may simply need to make an appointment. We're the leaders, and it always begins with us.

Leaders have a great responsibility to initiate healing so that relationships are clean. Healthy relationships give a church the power to change. If people believe in you and trust you, and if you respect and believe and trust them, change becomes much easier. You can't change a church when you're locking horns. When you *repair broken* relationships, the difficulty of change *decreases.* When you *undermine healthy* relationships, the measure of difficulty in change *increases.*

ealthy relationships give a church the power to change.

Miracles Stop When Relationships Are Broken

In Mark 6 we find Jesus teaching in the synagogue. "Many who heard him were amazed. 'Where did this man get these things?' they asked. 'What's this wisdom that has been given him, that he even does miracles! Isn't this the carpenter? Isn't this Mary's son and the brother of James, Joseph, Judas and Simon? Aren't his sisters here with us?' And they took offense at him" (vv. 2-3). Verse 5 tells us that He could do no miracles there except to lay His hands upon a few sick people and heal them "And he was amazed at their lack of faith" (v. 6).

I looked at that situation and thought, *If we take offense and we hold offense, then the miracles cease. Lord, I sure don't want You to come to our church and see all the offenses that we've tolerated between people and we don't speak to it. I'm just wondering, Lord, if You'd look and say, "I'm just amazed at your unbelief. You know, I'd like to do miracles here, but I can't. The soil is not conditioned."*

When I hold onto offenses, I release the presence of miracles. What happens is that resentment starts to take root, and the miracles of God are cut off. Heb. 12:15 says, "See to it that no one misses the grace of God and that no bitter root grows up to cause trouble and defile many."

When there is resentment, the grace of God can't move. The miracles of God cannot increase, because we would rather have offenses than miracles.

Do you want miracles? I do. I want to see transformed lives. We must see churches turn around and people released into ministry. That's why it's imperative that church leaders declare war on offenses and broken and snagged relationships and let nothing go underground. That's our responsibility.

Resentment is such a dangerous thing. It's like drinking poison and waiting for the other person to die. That happens all the time in our churches, because resentment kills me first before it kills anybody else. When there's resentment, people sabotage each other.

Will you lead the charge to restore broken relationships? If there's anything out of whack, will you deal with it? Start by asking your leaders, "Is there anyone we need to write a note to, starting with someone else in this room? Is there anything that's gone underground that shouldn't?"

Do it. Lead the way. Make it right. When you do, any program will fly.

Will you join me in the following prayer?

Lord Jesus, You've asked us to be the people of God, but not just in religious ways, because we understand that being religious alone is not enough to change the world. We need to be people who live out what Your Word is saying. Lord, help us to be a people of forgiveness. We pray for our churches, that You will allow this restoring of healthy relationships to happen in a great way. O God, let the cause of Christ be so great that nothing comes in the way of it. Lord, I ask that You restore our nation and restore our churches. Start with us inside this circle. Start with me. In the name of Jesus Christ we pray. Amen.

▪11▪

TAKING RISKS WITHOUT RISKING YOUR SOUL

The Pastor-Leader's Need for a Healthy Soul

Maxie Dunnam

I'm at the age when, hopefully, I can share a bit of experience or even wisdom for those who are beginning as well as those who have been at it for a while and have made the saving discovery that our calling and our performance in ministry require on-course adjustments all along the way. Years ago in my devotional journal I made this entry: "Let not your will roar when your power can but whisper." I discovered that quotation, by Thomas Fuller, in my devotional reading in May 1993.

Let me share a confession that will explain why this admonition has such meaning for me. I grew up in rather severe poverty in Perry County, Mississippi. My mother and father did not go to high school. I felt myself culturally, socially, intellectually, as well as emotionally deprived. In response, I developed an almost sick determination to achieve. The game I have played through the years is this: "See here—I am worthy of your love and acceptance."

Throughout my life, up until a few years ago, I had a recurring dream that expressed itself in different ways but always involved my being somewhere about to preach. Sometimes the service of worship was to begin in 10 minutes and I would be struggling to button the collar of my shirt or trying to tie my tie without success. Or I might discover that the cleaner had mixed up my clothing, and I would put on a pair of pants and find the coat didn't match. Or I might even discover that the pants were three or four inches too short.

The dream always had something to do with the drivenness of my life—all circling around my own feelings of inadequacy and unpreparedness.

Roars and Whispers

Though I had not had that dream for years, it happened again on Tuesday night, July 27, 1993—a date I recorded in my journal. When I woke at five in the morning, I was in a sweat and all worn out. It was the same old thing. In my dream, I had to preach at a big convention. I had not had time to make the kind of preparation I'm committed to make; I had just been too busy. I kept saying to myself, *Well, undoubtedly I'll get some time and can put something together.* But time was not given, and the evening for my speaking assignment arrived. I threw some sermon manuscripts into a file.

I grabbed the file and headed for the convention hall. I got there 15 minutes before it was time for me to preach. I went into the first available door and found myself in a coffee shop. It was a place where people with no commitments to be somewhere else gathered to talk. So I sat down at a table and began to go through the file to find something I could use that night.

Then I became aware that four men were sitting at a table over in a corner of the room. One of them recognized me, came over immediately, and introduced himself as a minister. He told me he had been reading my books and how much he appreciated my ministry. Instead of saying to him, "Look—why don't we have some time together after the service tonight?" I cut him off with some angry words about being interrupted.

In desperation, I returned to my effort to find something to say. Then it was time—time to go on. I grabbed some notes and started to leave the room and go to the podium. I had on a freshly starched white shirt and my best suit—so I thought. The truth was that I had my coat on, but I looked down and discovered I was wearing the pants of a jogging suit.

Then the dream ended, and I felt exhausted as I started my day.

I went to my study for my morning time of prayer after that dream, having received a message from God to surrender, to let go. In retrospect, I knew why I had that dream. I was overextended and stressed by a calendar I wrote. I was the chair of the Committee on Evangelism for the World Methodist Council, and I was supposed to leave that coming Sunday to visit a congregation in the Czech Republic, to speak at a conference in Estonia, and to visit a congregation in Russia. I was also chairing the Board of Trustees and Search Committee to help find a new president for Asbury Theological Seminary. I was working on a book manuscript that had a deadline four weeks later. A lot of things were going on in the life of our church—Christ United Methodist Church in Memphis. Opportunities for ministry were almost overwhelming. On top of all that, my mother had a stroke the Sunday afternoon preceding the dream.

So God was speaking to me again? I sure don't know, but the words from Thomas Fuller came alive again: "Let not your will roar when your power can but whisper."

I yielded and released the Lord's promises in my life. I canceled my trip to Russia. I told the Lord I was going to do my best to be a responsible chairperson for the Search Committee at Asbury but that I was not going to get overly stressed about it. I accepted the fact that it would not be catastrophic if I missed my book deadline, and I committed my mother to the Lord. I would continue to be the best leader I could for my congregation, but I was not going to carry the weight of it on my shoulders.

Surrender and Relinquishment

So I surrendered. I realized again how limited I am in my own strength and how dependent I am upon the Lord, how yielded I must be to Him if His power is going to be perfected in my weakness.

Now here's the kicker. A year after that dream, I became the president of Asbury Theological Seminary. It was not what I wanted, but I became convinced that it was God's will for this particular season of my life. How many times during my first years at Asbury did I recall Thomas Fuller's words: "Let not your will roar when your power can but whisper."

Hopefully, you are autobiographically on board with me now.

Let me make my case for the thesis of this chapter and then turn to several specific scriptural principles about soul risk. The heart of what I want to say to every church leader is that spiritual, emotional, and relational growth take time and energy. It requires discipline. Most ministers starting in ministry are so enthusiastic for God; they want nothing more than to be sterling men and women of faith. Whether it's due to our seminary training or ecclesiastical machinery or competition among pastors, it's not long into our ministry journey before we are tempted to become increasingly preoccupied with success. We start climbing the ladder, looking for a bigger church, a bigger salary, and greater recognition.

Out of Focus—and What to Do About It

We take risks, and we enjoy doing so. Risks can be good, as long as we don't risk our own souls in the process. Later in ministry, we might realize how we've strayed from those ordinal commitments. Somewhere along the way, most of us wake up to the fact that we've not kept an accurate perspective over the long haul. If we've not forsaken our first love, we certainly have not given it first place. Unfortunately, many of us are in our 40s and 50s before we come to this realization. All of us could recall the events and crucial time frames in our ministry that were watershed occasions, transition times, marking dramatic redirection or paradigm shifts in our understanding of vocation, church, the Christian life, and spirituality. One of those came for me when I was invited to join the staff of The Upper Room to direct a ministry, primarily calling people to a life of prayer, providing direction and resources for growth in and the practice of prayer. I told Wilson Weldon, then editor of *The Upper Room*, who interviewed me for the position, that the fact they were inviting me to assume this responsibility showed how desperate the church was since I was such a novice in this area of prayer life.

This new responsibility forced me to be even more deliberate and disciplined in my own personal life of prayer, but it also introduced me to a wider dimension of spirituality than I had known. During those days I knew no one within the Protestant tradition who was talking about *spiritual formation*. The Roman Catholics have known the importance of this aspect of Christian growth and have used "formation" language for centuries.

I became intensely interested in the great devotional classics. The Upper Room had published a collection of booklets— selections from the great spiritual writings of the ages, writers whose names I barely knew and to whose writings I was a stranger: Julian of Norwich, William Law, Francois Fenelon, Francis of Assisi, Evelyn Underhill, Brother Lawrence, and an array of others. I began a deliberate practice of keeping company with the saints, seeking to immerse myself in the writings of these folks that had endured through the centuries, expressing Christian faith and life and becoming classic resources for the Christian pilgrimage.

I began a deliberate practice of keeping company with the saints, seeking to immerse myself in the writings of these folks that had endured through the centuries.

As I have kept company with the saints, I've observed characteristics they had in common:
They passionately sought the Lord.
They discovered a gracious God.
They took Scripture seriously.
Jesus was alive in their experience.
They practiced discipline, at the heart of which was prayer.
They were convinced that obedience was essential for their life and growth.
They sought not ecstasy but surrender of their will to the Lord.
They were thirsty for holiness.
They lived not for themselves but for God and for others.
They knew joy and peace, transcending all circumstances.
I submit this incredible list to you as the dynamic that will enable you to stay alive in your ministry and guarantee that you will finish well. I want to elaborate on four.

1. They practiced discipline, at the heart of which was prayer.

Sister Marie Bonaventura was living a relatively relaxed life as a nun in Rome. After much encouragement, she was persuaded to attend a conference on the disciplines of the spiritual life. The very first meditation was on the purpose and end of man. It inspired such fervor in her heart that the priest, giving the meditation, had scarcely finished when she called him to her and said, "Father, I mean to be a saint, and quickly." She then went to her cell, and writing the same words on a scrap of paper, she fastened it to her crucifix, where it would be a constant reminder.

The saints have all known that there is no way "to be a saint, and quickly." St. Francis de Sales gave direction for our beginning journey:

> We must begin with a strong and constant resolution to give ourselves wholly to God, professing to Him, in a tender, loving manner, from the bottom of our hearts, that we intend to be His without any reserve, and then we must often go back and renew this same resolution (*A Year with the Saints*, 2)

One of the most inspiring models of discipline in the sports world is Tiger Woods. At age 21 he won the Masters Tournament—the youngest ever to win and by a record 12 strokes. Just recently he won the Master's for the third time—13 strokes under par. In an article on "How the Best Golfer in the World Got Even Better," Don Goodgame wrote,

> For a glimpse into the greatness of Tiger Woods, look past his runaway victory in the British Open at St. Andrews last month. Forget his triumph—also by a record margin—in the U.S. Open at Pebble Beach in June. And set aside his prospects for stomping the field in another major tournament, next week's PGA Championship at Valhalla. Consider, instead, what Woods did right after he dominated the 1997 Masters. He studied videotapes of his performance: blasting 300-yd. drives, hitting crisp iron shots right at the pins, draining putts from everywhere. And he thought, as he later told friends, my swing really needs great improvement.

Woods said during an exclusive interview, "I knew I wasn't in the greatest positions in my swing at the Masters." He continued, "But my timing was great, so I got away with it. And I made almost every putt. You can have a wonderful week like that even when your swing isn't sound. But can you still contend in tournaments with that swing when your timing isn't as good? Will it hold up over a long period of time? The answer to those questions, with the swing I had, was no. And I wanted to change that."

In other words, Woods, already considered the best by many of his peers, was gambling that he could get dramatically better—and was willing to do whatever he thought might help him someday surpass his idol Nicklaus as the greatest ever (*Time*, August 14, 2000, 57-58).

That's discipline. It is a challenge to every Christian. It's a special challenge to pastors-leaders. Anyone who has read the gospels knows that Jesus' call is to a "narrow way." He couldn't have made it clearer:

If any want to become my followers, let them deny themselves and take up their cross and follow me. For those who want to save their life will lose it, and those who lose their life for my sake will find it. For what will it profit them if they gain the whole world but forfeit their life? Or what will they give in return for their life? (*Matt. 16:24-26*, NRSV).

It is through spiritual discipline that we learn to be like Christ and live as He lived.

Paul also made it scathingly clear: "I appeal to you therefore, brothers and sisters, by the mercies of God, to present your bodies as a living sacrifice, holy and acceptable to God, which is your spiritual worship" (Rom. 12:1, NRSV).

I don't know a Christian in all the ages to whom we turn for teaching and inspiration who did not give himself or herself consistently to discipline and devotion. It should be obvious that we need to place the disciplines for the spiritual life at the heart of the gospel. The purpose of discipline is to enhance our relationship with Christ, to cultivate a vivid companionship with Him. It is through spiritual discipline that we learn to be like Him and live as He lived.

Sister Marie Bonoventura's commitment may have been genuine: "Father, I mean to be a saint"—but her time line—"and quickly"—is really laughable. We must start at the beginning and go through the middle. The *beginning* is, as de Sales said, "a strong and constant resolution to give ourselves wholly to God" and the *middle* consists of often going back to renew this same resolution.

2. They were convinced that obedience was essential for their life and growth.

We remember that word of Jesus: "Not everyone who says to me, 'Lord, Lord,' will enter the kingdom of heaven, but only the one who does the will of my Father in heaven. On that day many will say to me, 'Lord, Lord, did we not prophesy in your name, and cast our demons in your name and do many deeds of power in your name?' Then I will declare to them, 'I never knew you; go away from me, you evildoers'" (Matt. 7:21-23, NRSV).

We do have a right to ask, to seek, and to know the will of God; but once we know it, nothing but obedience will do. The saints of old sought to arrive at the place in their relationship to Christ that their one longing was to live and walk in a way that would please God and bring glory to God's name. They were convinced that obedience was essential to their life and growth.

Obedience meant abandonment. Jean-Pierre de Caussade wrote to one who depended upon his spiritual guidance that abandonment to God "is, of all practices, the most divine." Listen to him: "Your total abandonment to God, practiced in a spirit of confidence, and of union with Jesus Christ doing always the will of his father, is, of all practices, the most divine" (Robert Llewelyn, *Joy of the Saints: Spiritual Readings Throughout the Year,* 101).

What a simple yet profound expression of abandonment: "to be content with being discontented for as long as God wills or permits." Does this idea remind you of what apostle Paul wrote hundreds of years ago when he said, "I have learned to be content with whatever I have. I know what it is to have little, and I know what it is to have plenty. In any and all circumstances I have learned the secret of being well-fed and of going hungry, of having plenty and of being in need. I can do all things through him who strengthens me" (Phil. 4:11-13, NRSV).

Our spiritual formation is a dynamic process, a growing willingness, or even a willingness to be made willing, to say yes to God every day in every way possible—no matter what the circumstances may be. The more we pay attention to God, the more aware we'll become of the yet-to-be-redeemed areas of our life—and the more we'll need to abandon ourselves to the transforming power of the indwelling Christ.

Let me share what may appear mundane to undergird this profound truth. I make my own witness. My wife, Jerry, and I decided to purchase a condominium on the beach, which, in our thinking, will be our retirement home. Being a few years away from retirement, I became preoccupied with this process. My concern broadened to the implications of my age, the sense that I was nearing the end of my "active" ministry. All of our savings would have to be poured into making the down payment.

For about six weeks, I could hardly get my mind off this monumental decision we were trying to make. That decision in a sense became my "dominant desire." *And that preoccupation did affect my praying.* Staying centered during my daily prayer times was difficult. I found myself unable to be as concerned about others as I normally am. I realized that, since this was my dominant desire, I had to surrender it completely to the Lord. And that wasn't easy. Only after days of deliberately laying this whole issue before the Lord in prayer was I free of my total preoccupation with it.

Jesus made clear how essential abandonment is when He taught us to pray, "Thy will be done." There are two common ways we pray this prayer. Sometimes we wrestle *against* God. We receive intimations of something God wants us to do, some call—and we wrestle *against* God because we're not sure we want to respond. Or we come face-to-face with an issue of God's justice and holiness—and we resist. We don't want to do it.

Sometimes when we pray "Thy will be done," it is a declaration of submission in which we confess that we don't know what is best but we want God's will. We struggle, we wrestle, we stay in the presence of the Lord until our hearts are made tender and we're ready to trust God and surrender our will to Him.

My favorite story about Lourdes, the famous place of healing in France, has to do with an old priest who was asked one time by a newspaper reporter to describe the most impressive miracle he had ever seen there. The reporter expected him to talk about the amazing recovery of someone who had come to Lourdes ill and walked away well. "Not at all," the old priest said. "If you want to know the greatest miracle that I have ever seen at Lourdes, it is the look of radiant resignation on the face of those who turn away unhealed!" That's abandonment!—"thy will be done" as a declaration of submission, confessing that all we want is God's will—nothing more, nothing less, nothing other than.

> *In the divine school of obedience, we all know there's only one textbook—Scripture.*

There are three seeds which, when planted in the soil of obedience, produce the fruit of God's will in our lives: (1) Scripture study; (2) Christian conferencing, that is, deliberately and honestly sharing with godly persons for edification and discernment of God's will and guidance; and (3) divine conviction wrought by the Holy Spirit.

In the divine school of obedience, we all know there's only one textbook—Scripture. We also know there's only one model—Jesus. We know, too, and have experienced the way the Holy Spirit will plant a deep, deep conviction within our lives, calling us to go in a particular direction.

I want to talk about a resource of knowing God's will that I think we pay too little attention to—"Christian conferencing." Jesus promised that where two or three are gathered together in His name, He would be present with them. Conferencing with godly persons who love Jesus, who want God's will for their lives and for us, is a trustful and dependable way to seek God's will.

One of the most dramatic moves in my life was based on my

accepting God's will through Christian conferencing—it was concerning the call to be president at Asbury Theological Seminary. For months I would not even consider the possibility, refusing even to talk with the search committee. The Holy Spirit impressed upon my wife the notion that I should at least consider what seemed to be a clear call through the committee. So we did—but without clarity on my part. In desperation, really, I began a conferencing process with godly persons whom I loved and trusted, some with whom I had shared my Christian walk for 25 years. I knew they loved God. I was certain they loved me and wanted God's best for me.

It was through them that I discerned God's will. Since making the decision to accept the seminary presidency, I've had little doubt that I was in the center of God's will. Over and over again my calling to this ministry has been confirmed.

This is the deliberate discipline of Christian conferencing. Let me speak briefly about this discipline in terms of the dynamic of friendship. We will always know a lot of people, and in our pastoral roles we will share deeply with people. But I'm talking about friends deliberately chosen and cultivated. Jesus said to His friends, "You did not choose me but I chose you" (John 15:16, NRSV). We have to take the initiative. Three things are essential:

1. We have to deliberately choose.
2. We have to make time—often sacrificially.
3. We have to be self-revealing.

Friendship is worth whatever price you pay for it. Donald McCullough makes the case: "When we consider the blessings of God—the gifts that add beauty and joy to our lives, that enable us to keep going through stretches of boredom and even suffering—friendship is very near the top" (*Mastering Personal Growth*, 41)

McCullough goes on to remind us that friendship demands "the sacrifice of encouragement" and "the sacrifice of mercy":

> *The sacrifice of encouragement.* Helping another person maximize his or her gifts can be costly. As you encourage her to be all that she can be, you may be ensuring a place for yourself on the second team. As you encourage him to

scale the heights, you may eventually find yourself at a lower level of recognition.

Perhaps watching a friend succeed should be easy—
even joyous—but it can be difficult.

The sacrifice of mercy. A relationship between two different individuals—even the best of friends—will inevitably
suffer tensions and disagreements, perhaps outright anger.
. . . We grant mercy when we're willing to endure the other
person. Speaking of his relationship with Jack Benny,
George Burns said, "Jack and I had a wonderful friendship
for nearly fifty-five years. Jack never walked out on me
when I sang a song, and I never walked out on him when
he played the violin." We need to plan on listening to our
friends' gravelly voices and screeching violins. . . .

Occasionally a relationship gets beat up and stomped
in the dirt by something far worse than irritations; it can fall
victim to brutal betrayals. By forgiveness we commit ourselves to keeping the friendship alive regardless of the
wounds it has suffered (50-51).

You are not going to make it well without friendship.

Once we know God's will,
nothing but obedience will do.

Let's summarize how we know and follow the will of God
through obedience. As stated earlier, there's a general will of God
for all His children that we can, to a marked degree, learn from
the Bible. However, there's a special individual application of
God's will concerning each of us personally. This comes to us
only through the Holy Spirit. On these occasions, the Holy Spirit
plants solidly in our being certain convictions about God's will.
We dare not quench the Spirit. Yet, it is altogether in keeping
with God's direction that we test these convictions with Scripture and Christian conferencing. Our friends may play a big role
in this testing. Again, however, once we know God's will, nothing but obedience will do.

3. They sought not ecstasy but surrender to the will of the Lord.

In her strange and beautiful book *The Cloister Walk,* which is part memoir and part meditation, Kathleen Norris talks about the experience of becoming a Benedictine oblate. She said she knew two things: One, she didn't feel ready to do it, but she had to act, to take the plunge. Two, she had no idea where it would lead. Listen to a portion of Norris' confession:

> The fact that I had been raised a thorough Protestant, with little knowledge of religious orders, and no sense of monasticism as a living tradition, was less an obstacle to my becoming an oblate than the many doubts about the Christian religion that had been with me since my teens. Still, although I had little sense of where I had been, I knew that standing before the altar in a monastery chapel was a remarkable place for me to be, and making an oblation was remarkable, if not, incomprehensible, thing for me to be doing.

> The word "oblate" is from the Latin for "to offer." And Jesus himself is often referred to as an "oblation" in the literature of the early church. The ancient word "oblate" proved instructive for me. Having no idea what it meant, I appreciated its rich history when I first looked it up in the dictionary. But I also felt it presumptuous to claim to be an "offering" and was extremely reluctant to apply to myself a word that had so often been applied to Jesus Christ (xvii-xviii).

T he saints did not seek ecstasy but surrender to the Lord.

After making that confession, Norris told about the monk who was to be her oblate director—that is, the one who guided her studies of the rule—a period that was supposed to last a year but rambled on for nearly three. She spoke with appreciation for this spiritual guide who waited patiently for her to sort out her muddle. Finally she said to him, "I can't imagine why God would want me, of all people, as an offering. But if God is foolish enough to take me as I am, I guess I had better do it."

The monk smiled broadly and said, "You're ready."

That kind of submission was the ongoing concern of the saints. They did not seek ecstasy but surrender to the Lord. They knew that *submission* in the Bible is a *love* word, not a *control* word. It means letting another love you, teach you, influence you, shape you. On the human level, the degree to which we submit to others is the degree to which we will experience their love. Regardless of how much love another has for us, we can't fully appreciate it until we're open, vulnerable, and submissive.

The saints of the Bible experienced the same thing in relation to God. They knew that it's only when we cannot imagine what God wants with us, or what He might do with it—and certainly when we are humble enough to know that anything He does for us or with us is all grace—it is only then that we put ourselves in the position for the Holy Spirit to work within us.

While we are not to seek ecstasy but surrender, Paul weds the two in a remarkable way. Here is one example:

They went through the region of Phrygia and Galatia, having been forbidden by the Holy Spirit to speak the word in Asia. When they had come opposite Mysia, they attempted to go into Bithynia, but the Spirit of Jesus did not allow them; so, passing by Mysia, they went down to Troas. During the night Paul had a vision: there stood a man of Macedonia pleading with him and saying, "Come over to Macedonia and help us." When he had seen the vision, we immediately tried to cross over to Macedonia, being convinced that God had called us to proclaim the good news to them (*Acts 16:6-10, NRSV*).

Paul was not seeking an ecstatic experience, but he was open and responsive to the Spirit's working in his life. He followed what some would certainly label *ecstatic*—a vision of a man begging, "Come over to Macedonia and help us." Paul interpreted this vision as God's call to go to Macedonia and preach the gospel.

He went specifically to Philippi, the major city in the Macedonian region, a port city and easy to get to. Miraculous things happened there. Lydia, a Gentile businesswoman, was converted, and the Philippian church was established in her house. A slave girl was delivered of "a spirit of divination" and that led to Paul and Silas's being beaten and thrown into jail. There in jail the third miracle took place. While Paul and Silas were praying and praising God at midnight, God honored their trust and faithfulness by throwing open the prison doors and freeing them. This miracle led to the conversion of the jailer—all the result of Paul's surrender to an ecstatic vision.

The lesson is clear. When we're open to the Holy Spirit and cease trusting our own wisdom and power, our actions, and accomplishments will far exceed our normal potential and capacity as commonly perceived. Jean-Pierre de Caussade addressed the issue in this fashion:

> Those who have gauged the depths of their own nothingness can no longer retain any kind of confidence in themselves, nor trust in any way to their works in which they can discover nothing but misery, self-love and corruption. This absolute distrust and complete disregard of self is the source from which alone flow those delightful consolations of souls wholly abandoned to God, and form their unalterable peace, holy joy and immovable confidence in God only (*Joy of the Saints*, 249).

We need to keep balance: never trust our own resources alone, but never doubt that the Holy Spirit will use us, often in remarkable, even miraculous ways. Again, the key is to seek not ecstasy but surrender and openness to the Spirit's working.

I don't know a more crucial issue for any Christian—especially the pastor-leader. My hunch is that many of us—in fact, I would be so bold as to say *most* of us—have shut ourselves off from the Holy Spirit's power because we've seen too many excesses and distortions in Christian communities where the dominant emphasis is on the Holy Spirit. We're reserved in our consideration of and openness to the Spirit, because we guard against the ecstatic.

One of the most fantastic promises Jesus gave us was "He who believes in Me, the works that I do he will do also; and greater works than these he will do, because I go to My Father" (John 14:12, NKJV). If that is even remotely possible, then must not we admit that we've never taken Jesus seriously? The least we have to confess is that we've been satisfied with far less than Jesus had in mind for those who would be His followers.

"Greater things."

Note the phrase "go to My Father." What did Jesus say He would do when He went to the Father? He said He would send the Holy Spirit. And what would the Holy Spirit do? Another fantastic promise: "You will receive power" (Acts 1:8).

Let me ask you a question. When was the last time you attempted something so great, so demanding, so Kingdom-like that you knew you would fail unless you received the supernatural power of the Holy Spirit? That's risk!

When was the last time you heard the call of God to do something bold, and you followed boldly, knowing that the only way you would walk in the way you were being called was to be guided by the Holy Spirit?

Again, the key is not to seek ecstasy but to seek surrender and openness to the Spirit's working.

4. They were thirsty for holiness.

If there is no obvious difference between a Christian and a non-Christian, something's wrong—seriously wrong. Paul made a graphic distinction between those who belong to *the day* and those who belong to *the night:*

> But you, beloved, are not in darkness, for that day to surprise you like a thief; for you are all children of light and children of the day; we are not of the night or of darkness. So then let us not fall asleep as others do, but let us keep awake and be sober; for those who sleep sleep at night, and those who are drunk get drunk at night. But since we belong to the day, let us be sober, and put on the breastplate of faith and love, and for a helmet the hope of salvation. For God has destined us not for wrath but for obtaining salvation through our Lord Jesus Christ, who died for us, so that whether we are awake or asleep we may live with him. Therefore encourage one another and build up each other, as indeed you are doing *(1 Thess. 5:4-11, NRSV).*

See the sharp distinction between "children of light" and "children of darkness." What Jesus wants is not admirers but disciples—those who will conform their lives to His.

Meister Eckhart warned that "there are many who are willing to follow our Lord half-way—but not the other half" *(The*

Imitation of Christ, arr. and ed. Douglas V. Steere, Great Devotional Classics, 8).

All the saints acknowledged this. *They were thirsty for holiness* and sought to conform their lives wholly to Christ.

The end toward which we move in our thirst for holiness is purity of heart. The Puritan divines labeled this *heart-work.* John Flavel, a 17th-century English Puritan, put it in this perspective: the "greatest difficulty in conversion is to win the heart to God; the greatest difficulty after conversion is to keep the heart *with* God. . . . Heart-work is hard work indeed" (*Keeping the Heart,* 5, 12).

The crux of our heart work toward holiness is our will fully surrendered to Christ so that God can take full possession of us. The apostle Paul expressed it autobiographically:

> But if, in our effort to be justified in Christ, we ourselves have been found to be sinners, is Christ then a servant of sin? Certainly not! But if I build up again the very things that I once tore down, then I demonstrate that I am a transgressor. For through the law I died to the law, so that I might live to God. I have been crucified with Christ; and it is no longer I who live, but it is Christ who lives in me. And the life I now live in the flesh I live by faith in the Son of God, who loved me and gave himself for me. I do not nullify the grace of God; for if justification comes through the law, then Christ died for nothing (*Gal. 2:17-21,* NRSV).

Holiness requires the full surrender of our independent self-will in order that God can eradicate our self-orientation.

I have a young friend named Tammy Hutchins who is living this Jesus style dramatically. She was converted at the University of Georgia, in Athens, Georgia. She arrived at Asbury Theological Seminary, in Wilmore, Kentucky, as a student about the same time I came as president. I didn't learn her story, a modern faith miracle story, until a couple of years later. She arrived at school with only enough money to take her through the first semester. She worked as much as she could, but there was no way she could work enough to pay her tuition and living expenses. So she prayed. She never asked for money, but time and again when she had nothing, no money to continue, somehow it would come.

The summer before her last year in seminary, she went to India on a short-term mission. By a series of circumstances and following God's call, she returned to India a year later to establish "Kirubai Home," a home for street children. Kirubai is pronounced KEE-ROO-BAY and is the Tamil word for "grace."

When I last heard from Tammy, she had 37 children under her care in two different facilities. The story is the same as it had been during her years in seminary. She is totally dependent upon the Lord. Again, I have never known her to ask anyone for money, but miraculously she receives what she needs.

She sends E-mails to a number of her friends, telling the story of what's going on and the miracles that are taking place. Though Tammy is young—very young compared to me—I'm learning from her simple, bedrock faith and radical abandonment to Jesus. Always there is the confession of her dependence upon the Lord and her willingness to live sacrificially in order to fulfill God's call upon her life.

In an E-mail that came October 4, 2000, she wrote the following:

> I encourage you to let God take you deeper in prayer and intimacy. I know these are the "Christian catch phrases" these days. But . . . well . . . it's the truth. I guess my prayer for you is that you would go deeper with Jesus, that you would let Him wash through you like a rushing river, cleansing, soothing, filling you in every good way. Intimacy . . . just more of Jesus. That place where you utter a prayer, and in an instant you know it has been answered. That place where you are convicted of your self and sin and in the same moment encouraged and refreshed. That place in your heart where man's words cannot reach—but one word from God, and you melt.

Congregation Needs My Personal Holiness

Again let me share a part of my pilgrimage.

There are some experiences or encounters that are so solidly lodged in our memory they continue to invade our consciousness—to haunt us—to help us or to hinder our Christian walk, to call and challenge us to be more than we are.

John Birkbeck is a person around whom for me a whole

cluster of memories is gathered—memories that invade my immediate awareness now and then. John was a Scots Presbyterian preacher. During a part of my tenure as the world editor of *The Upper Room,* he was the editor of the British edition and was a marvelous preacher in the classic style of the Scots divines.

I remember long walks with him in the evenings through the streets of Edinburgh, Glasgow, and Aberdeen. I remember extended hours across a table in a café over coffee—talking and talking and listening and listening. We were never together without my probing him about Christian doctrine, his own insight into biblical truth and preaching, and the wisdom of the Scots divines. It was John who introduced me to the Scots preacher Robert Murray McCheyne. I hope I'll never forget what John brought to my attention in one of McCheyne's books. Listen to it: "The greatest need of my congregation is my own personal holiness."

Lodge that solidly in your minds. I found it true in all my years of pastoral ministry, "The greatest need of my congregation is my own personal holiness."

I remember a time in my life back in the early 1960s when I was confronted with this shocking fact: *I am as holy as I want to be.* I was a young Methodist preacher in Mississippi, the organizing pastor of a congregation who had known amazing growth. It was also in the midst of the civil rights upheaval in the South—and Mississippi, of course, was a constant powder keg.

The church was a kind of Cinderella story—a dramatic demonstration of church growth. It became one of the success stories of Mississippi Methodism. Back during those days we had no church growth literature. There was no testing of persons to see if they would make good candidates for church planting. We did it intuitively, "by the seat of our pants," as we would say down in Perry County, Mississippi. I worked myself to the bone and was often worn out physically and emotionally. I kept asking myself a lot of questions: "What's the difference between this congregation and the Rotary Club? Is there a quality of life here that's not present wherever people meet together? Why is it that most of these people have the same ideas about race relations that people outside the church have?" And on and on the questions went.

It was a tough time, and the fellowship of the church was splintered by my involvement in the civil rights movement. I didn't think there was anything radical about my involvement, but many folks in the church could not understand my commitment and participation. I couldn't understand their lack of understanding. The gospel seemed rather clear.

Do You Want to Be Holy?

The pressure, stress, and tension wore me out. I was physically, emotionally, and spiritually exhausted and ready to throw in the towel. I even had thoughts about giving up the ministry. My resources were no longer adequate. Then, one of those "God things" happened. You know the kind of experience I'm talking about—a signal occasion that sets us on another path or at least sends us in a different direction than we had been going.

I went to a week-long retreat/conference, a Christian ashram, led by the world-famous missionary-evangelist E. Stanley Jones. I will never forget going to the altar one evening to have Brother Stanley lay hands on and pray for me. He knew my story —we had shared together during the week. As I knelt, he asked me the probing question "Do you want to be whole? Do you want to be holy?"

That was a signal sanctifying experience in my life, changing forever the direction of my ministry. Through the years since then, I've constantly asked myself: Do I want to be holy? and I have constantly reminded myself that I am as holy as I want to be.

Listen, brothers and sisters, holiness is not an option for God's people. God's call is clear: "Be holy, because I am holy" (Lev. 11:44). I'm totally committed to the priesthood of all believers, and I'm seeking to move Asbury Theological Seminary from a clergy/mainline church paradigm to the ministry of the whole people of God paradigm. But hear me—that does not lessen the meaning and importance of ordination. We are called by God and set apart by the church as pastor/leaders and representative ministers—and as McCheyne reminds us, "The greatest need of my congregation is my own personal holiness."

Heart Lessons from Ezekiel

A couple of years ago I was smitten in my heart by a word I

heard in an ordination service of the Free Methodist Church. It was verses 4 and 5 of Ezek. 2: "The people to whom I am sending you are obstinate and stubborn. Say to them, 'This is what the Sovereign LORD says.' And whether they listen or fail to listen —for they are a rebellious house—they will know that a prophet has been among them."

Ezekiel is sharing his personal story of God coming to him in a vision and calling him to be a prophet/priest. He sees the glory of Yahweh coming down from heaven, and it is so overwhelming that he falls on his face. But the Lord will not let him remain there: "Son of man, stand up on your feet and I will speak with you" (Ezek. 2:1). And the Lord does speak. The message that Ezekiel is to preach is given to him in a kind of scroll. So he receives his appointment. It's not a promising situation. Not to plant a new church that's sure to grow in an exciting fashion. Not to be the senior pastor of First Church downtown, which has tremendous influence in the entire community. Not an appointment to a rapidly growing church in suburbia. It's a hard call, and God makes it clear. In exercising his prophetic office, Ezekiel will have to preach to deaf ears and dwell among scorpions. Now all of us have preached to deaf ears—but none of us have dwelt among scorpions—though one of our student pastors told me recently he had some polecats in his congregation. There is no prospect of success laid on the prophet in his initial call to ministry. And that burden of no prospect continues to increase as God continues to speak.

In this call of Ezekiel, we see some lessons, some directions, and powerful promises to us as we search to stay alive all our ministry life and as we seek to be holy as God is holy.

First, God says, "Stand up on your feet and I will speak to you" (2:1). The lesson? We're to listen. Our stance must always be a receptive one. "Speak, LORD, for your servant is listening" (1 Sam. 3:9).

Now note the second thing: after hearing God tell him to "stand on his feet" so that He might speak to him, Ezekiel says, "As he spoke, the Spirit came into me and raised me to my feet, and I heard him speaking to me" (v. 2). The lesson? It's not our ability to do what God calls us to do, but our willingness to respond, to yield, to attempt what He calls us to that releases God's power. God called Ezekiel, "Stand on your feet" but then—as Ezekiel says—"a Spirit entered in to me and set me on my feet" (NRSV).

We may express this second lesson in this way: God does not call us to a ministry or a mission that we can accomplish in our own strength and with our own resources—but only with His divine aid. In that way we're kept on our knees, dependent upon Him.

Then we find a third lesson and a promise. Listen to it:

> He said to me, "Son of man, eat what is before you, eat this scroll; then go and speak to the house of Israel." So I opened my mouth, and he gave me the scroll to eat. Then he said to me, "Son of man, eat this scroll I am giving you and fill your stomach with it." So I ate it, and it tasted as sweet as honey in my mouth (*Ezek. 3:1-3*).

The lesson? We must become one with God's word. What we say must be matched by how we live. It is then that people will know that a prophet is among them. That's what character and holiness are all about as they relate to our Christian vocation.

A Guarantee for Finishing Strong

Well, that's it—a lot of words from Scripture and the saints —hopefully enough autobiographical witness to confirm personal integrity and enough wisdom and direction to enable you to stay alive all your ministry life. It all comes with a guarantee— not a money-back guarantee but a life-back guarantee. If you pay attention to these lessons from the saints, you'll finish strong. Then when you take risks of faith, you'll know what you can risk without risking your soul.